THE HOLY WEDDING
CHRIST AND HIS BRIDE

KIM HUFF

ISBN 978-1-64003-820-2 (Paperback)
ISBN 978-1-64003-821-9 (Digital)

Covenant Books, Inc.
11661 Hwy 707
Murrells Inlet, SC 29576
www.covenantbooks.com

INTRODUCTION

Welcome to the Holy Wedding, a six-week study that is purposely fashioned for you, the studier, to mine for yourself the treasures found in God's Word. Each of these lessons will build on the previous one, so it's vital that you stay engaged. It may seem like a lot of work, but if you do a little each day, it's not all that demanding.

My heart's desire and prayer is that you seek God's presence as you come before Him each day and expect Him to meet you there to "tell you great and unsearchable things you do not know" (Jeremiah 33:3). I can't do that; I can only relay what He's shown me—don't be satisfied with that. Let God whisper truth to you personally as you sit before Him expectantly. I can confidently promise you that if you will, He will reward you with His presence, He'll speak to you personally, and He'll give you a hunger and thirst for more. I promise you, you don't have something more important to do. I unashamedly plead with you, do this and give it all you've got! My passion isn't for self-promotion but for you to allow God to enlighten the eyes of your heart to see Him and know more and more the wonder of His person. You can't get that from a teacher; it comes through seeking Him. So go ahead; taste and see that He is so good!

This study will reveal God's original intent to have a people in which He could share His love through an intimate relationship—like a marriage. We will pick up the thread of this beautiful picture in Genesis and follow it all the way through to Revelation, exposing from the very start God's design that would eventually lead to a holy wedding between Himself and His people. In order to fully understand the implications of this relationship, we will need to examine two things:

1. The elements of a Jewish wedding
2. The nature of a covenant

Jewish Wedding

The Bible uses imagery to convey meaning. The early writers and readers of the Scriptures viewed their world in concrete rather than abstract terms. Because of this, they used word pictures and stories instead of formal definitions to describe God and His relationship with his people. So while we, as Westerners, when asked to describe God, might say, "He's majestic, holy, righteous," a Jewish person would say, "He's like a shepherd. He's a rock. He is living water. He's a fortress."

The Bible also uses this imagery to describe the people of God. They (we) are described as sheep, soldiers, slaves, athletes, etc. But the most tender and affectionate way God refers to His people is as a bride (Isaiah 62:5, Jeremiah 2:2, Revelation 21:2).

To fully appreciate this analogy, it's necessary to understand the customs of a Jewish wedding and the elements involved in the marriage process. The customs of a wedding in biblical times hold very little resemblance to our present-day practices, so the illustration of the church as the bride of Christ can be unclear or incorrectly understood. But if we understand these traditions, the prototype paints a beautiful picture of Christ and the church.

The union of a Jewish man and woman in biblical times began with the betrothal. It was common in ancient Israel for a young man's *father to select a bride* for his son. In the situation where the father himself could not go to meet with the bride's family, a designated representative was sent as a marriage broker or matchmaker. A biblical example of this is in Genesis 24:1–4 when Abraham sends his servant to his brother's family in order to acquire a wife for Isaac.

When the bride was selected, the bridegroom and his father would then approach the potential bride and her father and present a *marriage contract, or ketubah*. This was actually more than a contract; it was a covenant agreement containing the provisions and conditions of the proposed marriage. Interestingly enough, the ketubah was essentially a statement of the husband's obligations; the obligations of the wife to her husband were not recorded.

In spite of the fact that the marriage was arranged, the consent of the bride appears to be an important part of the contract (Genesis 24:5 and 58).

After the marriage contract was settled, the *bride price* was then negotiated. Because the bride would be a significant loss to her family, the fathers of both the bride and groom would negotiate the bride price. The price would be set at a significant amount, and the groom would understand that he must pay dearly for the bride of his choice. In fact, the cost was often so great that the young man would seek the advice of his father as to the wisdom and prudence of the choice.

When both parties agreed, *the bride and groom would drink a cup of wine together, sealing the pledge.* This expressed the groom's willingness to sacrifice for his bride in paying the bride price; it also demonstrated the bride's willingness to enter into this marriage.

"From that moment, she was referred to as one who was 'bought with a price,' distinguishing her as an engaged woman" (followtherabbi.com, "Wedding Plans"). She would wear a veil whenever she was in public, signifying she was "set apart" for her bridegroom. It served as a visual division between her and any other suitor enabling others to know that she has been spoken for.

In preparation for entering into the formal betrothal period, the bride and groom separately underwent *a cleansing ritual or consecration (mikveh)*, which symbolized a spiritual cleansing.

After the consecration, the couple would appear under *the canopy, or chuppah*. Here the couple would publically state their intention to become betrothed or engaged. A cup of wine was shared to seal the vows. After this ceremony, the couple was considered to have entered into the betrothal agreement, and they were regarded as legally married.

The betrothal period is a time for the couple to then prepare to enter into the covenant of marriage. It is unlike our modern custom of engagement in that it is much more binding. A couple in the betrothal period would need a religious divorce in order to *annul the contract* (Deuteronomy

24:1–4), *an option only available to the husband.* At this point, the couple would live apart, and the marriage would not be consummated until the groom returned for his bride.

The couple would now part ways, but before he left, the groom would leave a *bridal gift* to demonstrate his commitment and to remind his bride during their separation of his promise to return. This gift was most often something to be used in preparation of the wedding.

The groom's responsibility was to begin *preparing a place for the new couple to live in his father's house.* In biblical times, a new house wasn't built for the couple, but additional rooms were added to the existing family home. These clusters of buildings were called *insulas.* They were built around a central courtyard where grandparents, aunts, uncles, and cousins all interacted together in community.

As with any new construction, the new addition would take some time, approximately a year. As much as the new groom may have desired to fling something together in order to hurry back to get his bride, the rabbi's stated that the new home was to be better than where the bride had previously lived (messianicfellowship.50webs.com). Therefore, the groom could not define when the work was complete; only the father could make that pronouncement. It was commonly understood that the construction project would take approximately a year, thereby giving a general awareness of a timeline, but the day and hour could not be known. *The father alone made the final assessment and determined when the groom could go and get his bride.*

The bride had her own responsibilities during this time. As she prepared to move away from her home and become a wife, her essential task was preparing her wedding garments. The wearing of a white dress had as much to do with spiritual purity as physical virginity. The bride would have a general idea of the time of her groom's return, but she could not know the exact day or hour. She was to be ready at any moment with her garments prepared and kept clean as well as her lamp outfitted with oil so that she would not be caught unprepared for her groom. The lamps would serve to both light the path before her as well as illuminate the face of her bridegroom.

When the time finally came, the groom would gather his friends and set out to claim his bride. Every attempt was made to completely surprise her—that was the goal—and "steal her away," so most often, they came at night.

It was customary for one of the groom's party to go ahead of the bridegroom with a shout, "Behold, the bridegroom comes!" The shofar would then be sounded. The groom and company would either gain entrance into the bride's home or she and her maidens would meet them as they approached. As she came out to meet her groom, her clean white garment indicated she was consecrated and prepared. The entire community would be awakened by all the commotion and would come out into the streets. The wedding procession would proceed to the house of the groom's father, and the groomsmen would again set up the chuppah, or covering, where the couple would repeat the sharing of a cup of wine and blessing as a remembrance of the betrothal ceremony.

After the ceremony, the couple would retreat alone into the bridal chamber. Although the couple is legally bound, the marriage was not recognized until the bride and groom had become one, so the groom's friend would stand at the door and wait for the bridegroom to tell him the marriage had been consummated. The friend would then announce to the wedding guests the good news that the couple was now united. The couple remained in the bridal chamber for a week. At the end of that time, they emerged to celebrate, and the marriage feast began.

The highpoint of the celebration was the marriage supper. After the festivities, the bride and groom lived together as husband and wife in the full covenant of marriage.

We will be coming back to discuss the fulfillment of this in a couple of weeks, so I don't want to say too much now and spoil it. But I'm sure as we've gone over the elements of a Jewish wedding, a number of things have captured your attention. For now, we'll move on to . . .

Covenants

Covenants were a familiar concept to the people of that time. It is widely understood that covenants did not originate with God. They were an established model He used to reveal something about Himself through. Covenants more closely resembled a marriage than a business agreement as a covenant bound the two parties together for life. The primary difference between a covenant and some other agreement was the relationship that was established.

Covenants were made between equal parties—those on the same socioeconomic level—in which specific promises were made by each party and the benefits and penalties were defined should the covenant be broken. In the case of a covenant agreement between unequal parties in which one participant was superior in power or wealth, the terms of the agreement were established by the superior person and could not be altered by the lesser person. "The lesser party could either accept the offer of relationship or reject it and exist in conflict with the greater party" (followtherabbi.com, "A Covenant Guarantee").

Covenants were not made but "cut"; you cut covenant with another. Unlike a contract in which both parties simply sign their names to a document; cutting covenant was physical, involving the sacrifice of animals. These animals were killed and split in half, creating a "blood path" between the two parts. Both parties would walk through the blood of the animals. Since blood is symbolic of life (Leviticus 17:11), the imagery was twofold:

1. They were merging their lives together.
2. They were promising to fulfill their part of the contract; otherwise, it would cost them their life just as the animal's life had been lost.

As you might expect, a covenant agreement was a very serious commitment that was never entered into lightly. To display the extent of the love and commitment God was vowing to His people, He entered into a covenant relationship with them.

God chose one man, Abraham, to set apart and create a people for Himself. He promised to make Abraham into a great nation, stating that "all peoples on earth will be blessed through you" (Genesis 12:3). To confirm His promise, God "cuts" covenant with Abraham.

Read Genesis 15:9–12, 17–18a.

The fire and smoke are both representative of God Himself; Abraham did not participate although the covenant was with him and his descendants. This was a unilateral covenant; God was taking responsibility for both sides. God would not fail in keeping His end of the agreement, and when Abraham and his descendants failed to "walk before me [God] and be blameless" (Genesis 17:1), God made Himself accountable.

The covenant made with Abraham was confirmed with his son Isaac; then Isaac's son Jacob. Some six hundred years later, when Abraham's descendants, Israel, is a large nation (as promised), God makes a covenant with them through Moses that looks much like a marriage covenant. It's the focus of this week's study.

The terms of the Mosaic covenant was specified in the Torah, or law. So if the Torah is God's covenant with Israel, the Ten Commandments are the summary document.

In general, ancient Near Eastern covenants had five sections: (1) the preamble, (2) historic prologue, (3) requirements, (4) blessings and curses, and (5) the summary documents. The covenant made at Mount Sinai contained all five sections. The following explanation was taken from followtherabbi.com, "A Covenant Guarantee" by Ray Vander Laan.

1. *The Preamble.* This section identified the two parties of the covenant. In the Torah, God established the identities of the parties in the creation story. He was the Creator, and Israel was his creation. In the covenant summary, the Ten Commandments, he said simply, "I am the LORD your God" (Exodus 20:2).

2. *The Historical Prologue.* In this part of the document, the history leading to the cutting of the covenant was recited to prove the right of the superior party to make it. In the Torah, the stories of the Fall, Noah, Abraham, and the Exodus are detailed as the basis for God's making the covenant with Moses on Mount Sinai. In the Ten Commandments, the summary is simply, "Who brought you out of Egypt, out of the land of slavery" (Exodus 20:2).

3. *Requirements (Commandments).* The Torah contains 613 of the requirements God placed on the people with whom He was in relationship. The number of obligations he placed on himself was even greater. In the summary of the commandments, these requirements were simplified to ten (Exodus 20:3–17). Some scholars have noted that Jesus reduced his summary to just two (Matthew 22:37–40).

4. *Blessings and Curses.* Keeping a covenant brought specific rewards, and breaking a covenant brought specific penalties. In the Torah, such blessings and curses are many and varied. Moses summarized both in Deuteronomy 28 in a powerful challenge to the Israelites. The summary document also contains curses and blessings scattered throughout the discussion of the requirements (see, e.g., Exodus 20:5, 7 for curses and Exodus 20:6, 12 for blessings).

5. *The Summary Document.* The summary document served two purposes. Because it was short, it could be easily read and stored. Because it summarized the entire covenant, it represented the total relationship between the parties. Normally, two copies of this document were made, and each party would take a copy to keep with them; it would be put it in a sacred place for safekeeping.

The Bible is silent about what was written on the tablets of the Ten Commandments, but based on the form that the covenant seems to follow in which two identical copies of a covenant must be made, it seems probable that each tablet would contain all ten commandments. One copy was God's, and the other belonged to Israel.

If this conclusion is correct, God made a profound statement by giving Moses both copies. It indicated that where He would dwell and His sacred place was the same as Israel's, the ark of the covenant in the holy of holies in the tabernacle!

Understanding the nature of a covenant in the ancient Near Eastern culture enables us to comprehend what an extreme choice it was for God to make in establishing a relationship with His people. That God Almighty, the great sovereign Creator, would make a covenant with a person or nation, binding Himself to them, was unheard of and incomprehensible! But by making this sort of pledge, He was stressing the degree of His love that will be fully realized in Christ (we'll get to that).

THE HOLY WEDDING

WEEK 1
"CHOSEN BY GOD"

DAY 1

Do you enjoy a good mystery? Most people do. A captivating story line and interesting characters engage us, and we enjoy following the story to the end, anxious to know how it all turns out. The Bible is like that. In fact, the New Testament alone uses the word *mystery/mysteries* twenty-seven times. These mysteries the Bible speaks of are not the same as our use of the word as a sequence of clues to provide the conclusion of a "who done it." It is an unfolding or revealing of things foretold, shadows of a future reality.

We are all familiar with the scripture that says, "'For my thoughts are not your thoughts, neither are your ways my ways,' declares the Lord. 'As the heavens are higher than the earth, so are my ways higher than your ways and my thoughts than your thoughts'" (Isaiah 55:8–9). I think we would all agree with this statement as it applies to God's intent for mankind. His thoughts and actions regarding man and His ways of accomplishing His great plan are nothing like what we would have devised. As the Bible begins to unfold the launch of God's good plan for mankind, we get only as far as chapter six of Genesis to find that it appears to be an epic failure. With the exception of a small few, humanity is destroyed. It will take the remainder of the Bible to reveal the great mystery of how God will finally produce a people for Himself.

Living in the era in which we find ourselves on God's kingdom calendar, we have the benefit of the almost completed tapestry of God's design for mankind. We've been given the privilege to perceive and understand what had been previously hidden.

It is a mystery so profound, it stirred Paul to make this statement in 1 Peter 1:12d. What did he say?

_____

Similarly, Solomon states that although God has set eternity in the hearts of men; finish the statement (Ecclesiastes 3:11):

_____

The mystery the Bible imparts from beginning to end is a truly beautiful love story chronicling a faithful, loving God's unending pursuit of a rebellious and unfaithful people.

The story begins for us in Genesis but not for God as He has no beginning. Before anything was created, God existed in a loving, joyful and complete company of three; the Father, Son and Holy Spirit. He is the eternal triune God who exists as love. He doesn't just show love; He embodies it. He _is_ love.

With this being true, a question naturally arises: as completely happy and fulfilled, why did God create man?

_____

God is all sufficient in Himself and has no unmet needs or desires; therefore, we give Him nothing in the sense that He may be dependent on us for anything. He is the giver and we are the receivers, "because he himself gives all men life and breath and everything else . . . for in him we live and move and have our being" (Acts 17:25b and 28a). But by its very nature, love has to be shared; it cannot be contained.

I read an analogy I found very helpful in understanding God's love and intent for man. Just remember that an analogy, especially as it concerns God and His ways, will be inadequate in some ways so focus on the aspects that help us.

> As a healthy couple is to birthing babies, so is God to creating humanity. It is an unhealthy couple who says, "Let's have babies so we will have someone to love us." "Let's have children so they will serve us." "Let's have children so we can boss them around." "Let's have children so we can get praise from their success."
>
> On the other hand, it is the healthy couple who says, "Because we have an abundance of love in our marriage, let's share it. Let's have babies who will look like us, have our life within them, and love like us. Then they can enjoy an intimate love relationship with us." It is this couple's pure love that motivates them to give children life.
>
> In eternity, I imagine God having a holy huddle and saying, "We have such a great life together and an overabundance of love, let's share it. Let Us make humanity in Our image so that they can love like Us. Then they can enjoy an intimate relationship with Us" ("Why Did God Create Humanity?" by Greg Brezina, Christian Families Today).

The perfect love of our triune God displayed itself in creating mankind so that man could participate in God's love by receiving, returning, and revealing it. God's desire was an intimate relationship with man and from the very beginning He starts to paint a picture. His design begins to emerge only in shadows:

> The man said, "This is now bone of my bones and flesh of my flesh; she shall be called woman for she was taken out of man." *For this reason* a man will leave his father and mother and be united to his wife, and they will become one flesh. (Genesis 2:23–24, italics mine).

God is ordaining and defining marriage in these verses. Adam is told that a man is to leave his mother and father and be united with his wife before there were any parents. In addition, God states, "for this reason" they were to be united.

What is the reason?

_____

In marriage, there must be a "leaving and cleaving." This new relationship trumps all other former alliances as a couple is joined together as one. Unity is the central principle in marriage.

Marriage was created by God as a display, a picture, of the kind of relationship He desires with His chosen people. We see from these verses a pattern developing; it's the first stroke of His brush on the canvas that will take thousands of years to complete.

Man's sinfulness spoiled God's intention. In the garden, Adam and Eve were accustomed to walking with God. They had open fellowship. When sin entered the world, the fellowship was broken, sin causing them to hide from Him. Shouldn't this have been the end? What was God to do with these two sinful, self-serving people? I'd say start over.

What did God say in Genesis 3:9?

_____

How fortunate for us the love of God is unfailing and enduring, therefore He pursues us. The pursuit is not a desperate attempt based on pride to regain what was lost, like a pathetic suitor, but a rock-solid commitment so enduring that it perseveres beyond sin or betrayal.

The Bible uses a word for God's unfailing love that is deeper and richer than anything we have in English; it is *hesed*. Hesed is a steadfast faithfulness based on a covenantal relationship that endures for all eternity. It is not just a feeling but an action with intent to restore brokenness and offer forgiveness. It is used 253 times in the Old Testament. It's translated as unfailing love, mercy, kindness, lovingkindness, and goodness.

Hesed is a love that goes far beyond the thrill of romance providing the security of faithfulness; it can be counted on day after day, year after year. Picture in your mind an old couple bent with age and unsteady walking hand in hand; that's hesed.

Cite some of your own examples of hesed:

_____

_____

_____

Hesed is the kind of love couples are agreeing to in their wedding vows: in sickness and in health, for richer or poorer, until death do us part, etc. Unfortunately, lifetime loyalty is very rare in our society, making hesed difficult to grasp.

God Himself proclaimed His great hesed in Exodus 34:6–7a. Write it here and circle the words translated from *hesed* (FYI, there are two), beginning with "The Lord, the Lord,

_____

_____."

Since hesed is the love God has, He continues with His plan for intimacy with His people. The earth became filled with many nations (Genesis 10:32 and 11:8–9), and God chose from all the nations that now exist a man to begin/create/originate/form a nation for Himself.

> "The Lord had said to Abram, 'Leave your country, your people and your
> father's household and go to the land I will show you. I will make you into a
> great nation and I will bless you; I will make your name great, and you will be a
> blessing. I will bless those who bless you, and whoever curses you I will curse; and
> all peoples on earth will be blessed through you'" (Genesis 12:1–3).

God enters into a covenant relationship with Abraham and tells him that his descendants will be mistreated slaves in a foreign country for four hundred years (Genesis 15:13). Fast forward to Exodus 1:8–14. As God stated, Abraham's descendants, Israel, have become a large nation of people, so much so that they posed a threat to the Egyptians. As a result, they are enslaved, oppressed, and mistreated. Enter Moses, whom God will use mightily to bring about Israel's liberation.

An important note: Much of what we are about to look into has been gleaned from the outstanding knowledge of a favorite teacher of mine, Ray Vander Laan, more specifically his study entitled *Fire on the Mountain*. He has a wonderful website, followtherabbi.com, as well as excellent DVDs on a number of subjects that I highly recommend. I will probably refer to him as RVL for the sake of convenience since it will no doubt be frequent. I mention this for a couple of reasons. First, I never want to assume credit for the wisdom of another; secondly, my aim in Bible study is to inspire others to dig into the wealth of fabulous information available. The same Holy Spirit indwells every believer, and His purpose and delight is to guide us into all the truth (John 16:13).

Back to our study. Read Exodus 6:5–8.

God tells Moses (Exodus 6:5) that He has heard the cries of the Israelites and has remembered His covenant with them. He goes on to state all the things He's planning to do for Israel, His part in the covenant. These are known as the "I will" statements of God. As He promises He will, God brings about a great deliverance for the Israelites.

Read Exodus 14:19–31.

From 14:31b, what two things occurred with the Israelites because of this experience?

_____

We should never lose the wonder of this mind-blowing event; it is to our benefit to try and imagine being in their sandals. What did it sound like when the invisible barrier pushed back the water making two massive walls? Was it a single person who took that first brave step forward or a group? As they walked, did they reach out to touch the water? Did they see fish (looking every bit as perplexed as they were!) in the wall of water on either side? Was there salty spray in their faces as they walked? Did they walk fast, anxious about how long it would hold? Put yourself there and imagine the sights, sounds, smells, etc. What a monumentally awesome experience and a major faith-building event.

Read their song of praise to God in Exodus 15:1–18.

In verse 2, they praise and exalt God for being their _____.

How do they describe themselves in verse 13?

_____.

What word do you suppose *unfailing love* is translated from in verse 13?

_____.

In verse 16c, the people describe themselves as _____.

This description is even more pronounced in 16d; what's the distinction?

_____.

God has set apart this group of people, this nation, as His own. Regarding this, Moses asks a question in Deuteronomy 4:32c. What does he ask?

_____

After the events at the Red Sea, God leads them through tremendous trials in the desert—bitter water, lack of food, no water, and fierce enemies. He reveals Himself as patient, attentive, and able as He provides for every need that they have.

What description does Jeremiah 2:2 use to show how Israel followed God in the wilderness?

_____

DAY 2

Now the picture that began in Eden starts to take some shape. As the people of Israel come to Mount Sinai, God will make a covenant with them. The Creator begins to unveil His plan to come down from heaven, establish an intimate relationship with His people, and live with them. This covenant God establishes with His people so closely resembles a marriage that later prophets described it that way. The events of Mount Sinai represent something far more significant than meets the eye.

Exodus 6:6–7 state God's covenant promises to Israel. What does the final one (Exodus 6:7a) say?

_____.

The word translated as *take* is often used when describing the action of taking a wife (Genesis 4:19; 11:29; 12:19; 21:21; 24:4, 7, 40, 48; 25:1, 20; Exodus 2:1; 6:6; Jeremiah 29:6). This is a wedding expression; it speaks of intimacy.

How does God describe His experience with Israel in the wilderness (Exodus 19:4c)?

_____.

I hope those words truly affected you. "I . . . brought you to myself." It's an exquisite picture of marriage; it's marriage language. We first heard it in Genesis 2:22 in the original marriage: "And he brought her to the man."

What does God tell Israel they will be to Him in Exodus 19:5?

_____.

The language God is using is personal and intimate. The relationship He was seeking with Israel went beyond a legal union; it inferred a marriage that would take place at Sinai. We don't know if what happened at Sinai became the pattern for future wedding customs for the Israelites or if He used current cultural rituals to communicate His intent. What is clear is that then as well as still today, "Jewish tradition views it as a 'wedding ceremony' where God betrothed himself to his people" ("Irony in the Extreme," Lois Tverberg, egrc.net).

Let's look at the elements that lead to this conclusion. Read Exodus 19:1, 20:17 and look for any characteristics you would expect to find at a Jewish wedding and list them here:

_____.

In Exodus 19:10 and 14, the people of Israel are told to consecrate themselves before they met with God, the same way a Jewish bride takes a ritual bath or the *mikveh* to prepare herself for her wedding. God is holy, and He requires holiness from His people (Leviticus 11:44–45, 19:2). To show the seriousness of the encounter, they were to prepare for two days by washing their clothes, abstaining from sexual relations, and confining themselves to the camp. There was no inherent merit in these actions; they were external expressions to show an inward act of sanctification, demonstrating the significance of meeting with God.

God tells the people, via Moses, that He will be coming to them on the third day (Exodus 19:11) in a dense cloud (Exodus 19:9).

Read Exodus 19:16–19. Where was the thick cloud (verse 16)?

_____.

Verses 19:18 and 24:15 tell us Mount Sinai was _____ in smoke. The covering of God's presence provided on Mount Sinai as He brought Israel to Himself is the basis for the chuppah (covering or canopy) used in traditional Jewish wedding ceremonies.

Where does Exodus 19:17 say they stood?

_____.

"This common translation communicates where the Hebrews were, but it does not capture the nuance of the Hebrew word that also implies being *under* or *beneath*. So the Jewish interpretation sees Israel as not just standing at the base of the mountain but standing under God's great chuppah as represented by the cloud. The chuppah symbolized God's desire to choose the Hebrews out of all the nations and bring them into an intimate relationship with himself" (Fire on the Mountain, RVL, pg. 221).

The Ten Commandments could be viewed as the *ketubah*, or wedding contract, the document specifying the commitment the bride and groom were making to each other in the covenant of marriage. They are the equivalent of wedding vows.

The most essential component of any wedding ceremony is the vows. The couple vows or pledges to do or not do certain things in their commitment to each other. These are posed in question form with the expected response being "I do" or "I will," depending on how it's asked.

Read Exodus 6:6–8. What were God's vows to Israel (what did He vow to do)?

_____.

How does He preface each statement; with what two words?

_____.

Read Exodus 19:3–6. What was Israel's vow to God?

_____.

What did they say (three times) in Exodus 19:8; 24:3, 7?

_____.

God spoke the Ten Commandments and continued to give the law in its entirety to Israel (Exodus 21–23). When the covenant is ratified, God calls Moses to the top of the mountain in order to dictate the specification for the tabernacle where He would dwell among them—the *bridal chamber* (Exodus 25:1—31:11). Exodus 25:8 says, "Then have them make a sanctuary for me, and I will dwell among them."

Israel would have a place where they could meet with God. The evidence of a wedding at Sinai is readily seen. Note the terminology the prophets use to describe the relationship between God and His people:

Isaiah 54:5 – "For your Maker is your _____, the Lord Almighty is his name."

Jeremiah 3:14a – "Return, faithless people," declares the Lord, "for I am your _____" (Jeremiah 3:14a). (ESV uses *master*, but it is the same Hebrew word as the one referenced above and below.)

Jeremiah 31:32d – "Though I was a _____ to them."

Hosea 2:7b – "Then she will say, 'I will go back to my _____ as at first, for then I was better off than now.'"

Hosea 2:16 – "In that day," declares the Lord, "you will call me 'my _____; you will no longer call me 'my master.'"

It would be incorrect to think these elements were pulled out to make the comparison when the reality is that God wanted this to be the portrayal all along; He put the components there.

If Sinai is perceived as a wedding, then the liberation from Egypt and many weeks in the desert would be considered the courtship between God and Israel (Exodus 15:22—17:16). God showed Israel the kind of husband He would be by parting the sea, sweetening the water, supplying the manna, providing water, and imparting strength for victory over their enemies. On the other hand, this experience exposed Israel as a grumbling, resistant group of malcontents. It's difficult to grasp why God would be interested in moving forward with this group! I would venture to say if any of us had a courtship like that, we would be branded as Bridezillas and our groom would be long gone . . . and rightfully so!

God has shown Israel faithful and committed love (hesed). In spite of her complaining, Israel must have developed a deep responding love to her Groom at this point. That being said, we could surely expect her encounter with God at Mount Sinai to be met with the kind of excited anticipation that all brides have on their wedding day.

With this picture in mind, consider God's emotions at this time. He is the groom after all, and for whatever reason, this is the bride of His choosing. What would you suppose some of His sentiments might have been?

Does it seem odd or difficult for you to think of God this way? Perhaps it seems inappropriate, irreverent or even sacrilegious. The Bible indicates that God shows emotion; He shows anger, hate, love, joy and jealousy to name a few. It's vital that we see God in these terms; His passionate love for His people is the only explanation for His patience and perseverance toward us.

Keep in mind it was God's idea to portray His union with Israel as a wedding, so there is no reason not to see Him as you would any other groom standing at the altar, eagerly awaiting His bride. Many people state that watching the face of the groom as the bride walks down the aisle is their favorite part of a wedding ceremony. Much is expressed on his face at that moment! Why wouldn't God have just as much love, excitement, and delight as His bride approached Him? It's important to stop and consider the tender emotions of God toward His people because we often default to an incorrect notion about His nature and His motives.

The meeting of God and Israel at Sinai is sometimes (might I say often) viewed as a frightful encounter with an angry God who's produced a list of demands that convey an "obey or else" attitude. I will admit that for many years I equated this scene to that of Dorothy and friends in front of "the great and powerful Oz." You remember it; they stand before the thunderous, loud, and intimidating Oz in knee-knocking, fingernail-biting terror. However, that is not at all the correct way to interpret the situation. Sinai was indeed frightful but only in the sense of awe and wonder. God's presence is sensational; He cannot help but make a spectacle! Israel considered it a marvelous event that this great and mighty God would come down and meet with humanity and speak to their nation personally (Deuteronomy 4:33–36).

DAY 3

Israel's view of the covenant agreement, the Ten Commandments, went beyond it being a legal code, a blueprint for correct conduct, and the beginning of God's Kingdom that would extend across the world for centuries. It was all of those things, but it was more than that; they were the wedding vows given to show Israel how to love God. RVL states that Jewish people dance when the Ten Commandments are read because they understand them to be more than dos and don'ts. They recognize them as God saying, "I love you."

What is your general attitude regarding the Commandments? How do you perceive them?

_____

_____

Does understanding God's sentiment behind them change your attitude?

_____

Rather than regarding the Ten Commandments as harsh demands from a displeased God, what if we perceived them as wedding vows inspired from a heart of pure, untainted, vibrant love? How had God shown Israel His love and deep commitment to them (Exodus 19:3–6 and Deuteronomy 7:6–9)?

_____.

What was Israel's part of the covenant (Exodus 20:1–17)?

_____.

This is what God was asking Israel to vow:
I am the God who loved you, rescued you from slavery and brought you to myself, therefore:

- You are to have no others, not in any form or fashion.
- I've given you My name; use it well, not in vain.

- Make time for Me.
- Since all of Israel is the bride, love and unity must be apparent among you:
    o Honor, treasure, and value your parents.
    o Don't harm others, take from them, lie about them, nor crave what they have.

If they were wedding vows (ketubah), they might sound something like this:

"Will you, Israel, forsaking all other gods, promise to love and cherish the Lord your God and have no substitutionary affections? Will you promise to honor the name you have taken and agree to conduct yourself according to the oneness of this union? Will you take Him to have and to hold in every good, as well as trying, circumstances by upholding intimate time together?"

How is it we deem the promises pledged in a modern-day wedding as beautiful and appropriate but regard the Ten Commandments that are so similar in nature as impersonal rules and regulations? It surely comes from a misinterpretation of God's motivation. We would benefit greatly to ask Him to enlighten the eyes of our hearts to perceive, recognize, and understand the depths of the intimacy He desires with us.

God is the lawgiver, but He places His law in the environment of grace. God saved and set Israel apart by His grace; they did nothing to bring it about. Mount Sinai is not where Israel came to become His people; that already happened at the Red Sea. Sinai is where they came to learn how to love God. His love language is obedience, and that's what He looks for in His bride. We cannot turn God's commandments into legalism; it's not legalism but love. We can and should tell God we love Him, but He wants to *see* it just as any husband desires their spouse to show love. God does not demand obedience for the purpose of making us His own; rather, it is because we *are* His that obedience is expected. Obedience is not a burden as if by it we earn a relationship with God; it is a grateful response, a display of love to our faithful God who has proven His love for us and established the relationship.

God desires to live with His people; He always has. What does He tell Moses in Exodus 25:8–9?

_____.

In the beginning, God created a space for mankind and told them to fill it. Unfortunately, what we filled it with was sin. Now God instructs the people to create the space, and He will fill it—with Himself! We often forget or neglect to understand the immensity of this offer.

How is God described in 1 Timothy 6:15–16?

_____

_____.

How is He described in Isaiah 57:15? (Write KJV if possible.)

_____

This God who is holy, holy, holy, who fills the whole earth with His glory, whom the highest heavens cannot contain, desires to live among them! We should be struck anew by His love and desire for intimacy with His people. A dwelling place for God would not be an easy undertaking. The tabernacle was very important to God; the Bible dedicates fifty chapters to creating it. The creation of the world only has two! Moses was gone for a long time, forty days, receiving the specs for the bride and bridegroom's first house together. In the meantime, Israel has become impatient, and what she does next is comparable to a bride having an affair on her honeymoon!

What had Israel specifically agreed they would not do (Exodus 20:3–6, 23)?

_____

What did they do (Exodus 32:1–4)?

_____.

Read Exodus 32:1–6. What was the specific purpose of the idol the people demanded (verse 1b)?

_____.

In giving Israel the law, how did God identify Himself (Exodus 20:2)?

_____

How had the Israelites received this statement; in other words, how did they know He said it (Exodus 19:9, 20:1; Deuteronomy 4:33, 36)?

_____.

What erroneous claim did they make about their new "god" (Exodus 32:4c)?

_____.

How interesting; this "god" that had not even existed the day before was now worshipped as the one who brought them out of Egypt! How do they refer to Moses in Exodus 32:1c?

_____.

In looking up this verse in every major translation, I found that, without fail, the word *this* was present—*this* Moses or *this* fellow Moses. Do you find that odd? Why would they describe him in this way?

_____

It appears to me that they want to distance themselves from Moses, perhaps to justify their actions. Look back at Exodus 19. What does verse 9 say was God's purpose in enabling the Israelites to hear Him?

_____

The verse (Exodus 32:1) also states that Moses "brought us up out of Egypt," but there is no mention of God who had lead them this far, and they knew it! They knew it was Him who brought them out of Egypt, who provided for them in the desert and manifested Himself before their eyes on the mountain; yet rather than waiting during this time of uncertainty, they decide to create a god themselves to "lead" them the rest of the way into the promised land. As preposterous as it seems that Israel would propose such a thing, it was even more so that Aaron would agree!

Read again Exodus 24:9–11. Who was on the mountain, and what did they see?

_____

Remember the song of Moses that all of Israel sang as they stood on the other side of the Red Sea. Read it again in Exodus 15:1–18. They do not appear to be the least bit confused regarding who they should credit for the astounding deliverance. What do we make of this? How did it go so wrong so quickly?

I believe the words they chose (Exodus 32:4c) are very telling. Perhaps they were not completely disregarding God but rather thought He had brought them this far and it was time for them to figure the rest out for themselves. They were probably thinking of the verse that says, "God helps those who help themselves." (By the way, where is that verse? I couldn't find it anywhere!)

The culture they had come out of had a god for everything—a god of fertility, the sun god, the moon god, etc. The god that was sought was determined by the need that they had. I'm certainly not interested in making excuses for them, but it's helpful to remember that they had been enslaved in Egypt for four hundred years. Egypt had many gods that had clearly influenced their thinking. I could be completely wrong about this, but it appears their actions were not necessarily disassociating themselves from God as much as they were adding Him to a list of gods. Nothing else makes much sense to me. The things they witnessed by God's hand were astounding; you don't forget those easily. I believe their confession on the shore of the Red Sea, as well as their assent to the covenant on

Mount Sinai, was sincerely spoken. Aaron himself had been among those who went on the mountain. Do we seriously imagine that forty short days could negate that?

It looks as if Aaron's actions may give some weight to this argument. When the people demand the god, what does Aaron tell them to do (Exodus 32:2)?

_____

What does God ask of the Israelites in order to construct the tabernacle (Exodus 25:3)?

_____

What does Aaron do in Exodus 32:5?

_____

What had God told them to do in Exodus 20:24?

_____

Aaron also announces to the people of Israel a festival in celebration of the new god (Exodus 32:5). Who is the festival "to"?

_____

Was this all an attempt by Aaron to soothe his conscience for what he had just done, hoping that by throwing in some "God stuff," God might be appeased? Or was he supplementing the gods of Israel? Aaron's actions seem very odd, given the circumstances. But don't we do the same thing?

Have you ever taken matters into your own hands when God has not immediately acted according to your expectations? What were the circumstances?

_____

_____

We are really no different from these rock heads and should be just as appalled at our own independent behavior as we are of theirs.

DAY 4

The problem appears to be Israel just didn't know God yet. They didn't know who He really was. We saw it displayed from the Red Sea to Sinai. Every time a new need arose, they began to worry, complain and grumble, indicating a concern that their current emergency would be too much for God. God would prove Himself in every situation, no matter what it was, to be competent. They simply could not grasp that this God was all-sufficient, all-powerful, all-encompassing, one of a kind.

God knew this would be an issue for Israel as He states His intention in Exodus 6:2–3 to reveal His character and nature in a fresh way. In the past, the patriarchs had known God as El Shaddai, God Almighty, All-Sufficient One. Now He would show them His character by the name Yahweh, Jehovah, or the LORD.

In biblical times, a name represented a person's character. God has many names in the Bible (i.e., Shepherd, Healer, and Provider), each one revealing His nature or an attribute; His name expresses who He is. It's important to notice the context in which He uses His name as they are always perfectly timed for the situation. When we know God by His name, all of them, we will be confident in everything that He is; we will have faith.

What does Proverbs 18:10 say about the name of the Lord?

_____

Every need God met for them in the wilderness was intended to reveal His sovereignty as well as His deep, long-suffering, determined love. This God was not like any other, and there would be no need for another; this relationship was to be exclusive. It would turn out to be a difficult lesson for Israel and the rest of us as well.

The celebration going on as part of the "festival to the LORD" was more than a party with eating and drinking. The words used speak of gross immorality; it was a drunken orgy. How ironic that God's bride was unfaithful to Him by creating and worshipping an idol, then celebrated that by having sexual relations.

God reveals to Moses all that is going on in the camp of the Israelites. What does He say in Exodus 32:7?

_____

_____.

What does God's choice of words regarding Israel tell you about His feelings toward them?

_____

It would not be an exaggeration to view this scene as a new groom returning from house hunting for their new home and finding his bride committing adultery; it would be an outrage! We would fully expect him to leave. In that context, what would you understand His emotions would be at this point?

_____

We have to know based on God's profound love for Israel that He was terribly hurt by their unfaithfulness. It's critical for us to keep in mind that sin grieves and saddens God; it causes Him pain. We would do well to grasp the sorrow and hurt we cause the Lord in our sin. I think if we genuinely understood God's true emotional reaction to sin, we would do things differently—as we should.

We must also remember He is a just God whose righteous anger burns against sin in our lives. In spite of His unfathomable love for His people, sin has consequences.

What is God's intention toward Israel (Exodus 32:9–10)?

_____

Moses intercedes on behalf of the Israelites (Exodus 32:11–13). What characteristics of God did Moses make his plea?

_____

What was the result of Moses' appeal (Exodus 32:14)?

_____

Moses comes down from the mountain as God instructed, "with the two tablets of the Testimony in his hands." How are the tablets described in Exodus 32:15b-16?

_____

_____.

Moses saw for himself the disgusting exhibition of the people, and Exodus 32:19 says he was

_____.

What did Moses then do?

_____.

This action was not just a fit of temper; it was symbolic of Israel breaking their covenant with God. When a covenant was broken, the offended party would publicly shatter the tablets that the terms were written on as a physical sign that the agreement had not been upheld. Israel has broken their covenant with God. By the very nature of a covenant agreement, this should have cost them their lives; they had to have been aware of that.

Exodus 32:25 states that the people had cast off all restraints, doing whatever they wanted. They were out of control and a laughingstock to their enemies. This is a picture of the outcome when the words of Judges 17:6 are true. What does it say?

_____.

Where does Proverbs 14:12 say this mentality and behavior leads?

_____.

Moses's presence and the broken tablets should have been a sobering event. But it's difficult to determine from the text if any of them even noticed. However, the penalty for their sinful unfaithfulness was about to fall and it would be great; "about three thousand of the people died." Moses once again intercedes. What was the purpose of this second intercession? God had already given His word not to destroy Israel. What was he seeking from God on Israel's behalf (Exodus 32:31–32)?

_____.

The text does not state that God answered the request (Exodus 32:33–34). What assumption do you make based on His words in verse 34 regarding His answer?

_____

_____.

God clearly plans to fulfill His part of the covenant for Israel to possess the land He has promised. However, there will be a change of leadership. From Israel's mass exodus from Egypt to now, God has led them. They had experienced unrivaled supervision and protection, but because of their actions, the result was the removal of His manifest presence. He will fulfill His promise, but He will not go with them. This brings up an obvious question. We know God is omnipresent, so how would that be possible for Him not to be present?

_____

God is present everywhere at all times, but the presence He's referring to here is a manifest presence. Wayne Grudem in his book *Systematic Theology* (yes, I own this book, and yes, I have to take a couple of aspirin after reading it) explains it this way: "God is present in every part of space with his whole being, yet God acts differently in different places. Furthermore, when the Bible speaks of God's presence, it usually means his presence to bless" and "When the Bible talks about God being 'far away' it usually means he is 'not present to bless.'"

Regarding this same issue, James MacDonald says, "While He is present everywhere in the universe, upholding and sustaining His creation, He is working actively only where He wills it so" (Vertical Church).

A couple of words are a considerable help in understanding this more clearly. Exodus 33:11 says, "The LORD would speak to Moses face to face, as a man speaks with his friend." Verse 15 says, "If your Presence does not go with us, do not send us up from here." The word translated as *face* (verse 11) and *presence* (verse 15) are the same Hebrew word. The absence of God's presence means Israel would be forfeiting the active and continuous intimacy they had been experiencing as His beloved, His treasured possession. The face-to-face relationship, as pictured in scripture between Moses and God, would be lost.

Perhaps the Israelites had grown accustomed to the manifest presence of God and were no longer in awe; familiarity had caused them to disregard the wonder of Almighty God in their midst. We know what familiarity breeds—contempt. Why that is so, I don't know, but I can attest from my own life that it is. God's goodness and favor can be the very reason we find ourselves imposing on His grace! Our cry and desire should be that of David's.

Read Psalm 27:8–9 and write verse 8 here:

_____.

The New Living Translations says it this way, "My heart has heard you say, 'Come talk with me.' And my heart responds, 'LORD, I am coming.'" What a compelling invitation. Spending time in the presence (face) of God should not be obligatory, but a delight. If we view it as mandatory, as in a daily staff meeting, then something's very wrong. This is the God who loves us, delights over us, and is willing to disclose great and unsearchable things we do not know! That sounds much more exciting than a staff meeting! If this is not your experience, then ask God that it would be. Ask Him to enable you to delight in Him as He delights in you.

DAY 5

Sin always causes a withdrawal of God's presence. Read Isaiah 59:1–2. What do these verses confirm about the effects of sin?

_____.

How does God continue to refer to Israel in Exodus 33:1?

_____.

Have you noticed the verbal tug of war going on between God and Moses regarding whose people the Israelites are? What is the reason God gives for His detachment from Israel (Exodus 33:3b, 5b)?

_____.

We could easily get the impression from His decision that He's being mean, maybe even vindictive; His attitude being, "Fine, you think you've got this? Knock yourselves out 'cause I'm done!" It would be the attitude of any normal person. However, we cannot substitute perceived truth for biblical truth and read into the text a human point of view. God always operates from love (because He is love) in spite of any emotion He may have. His decision not to go with them is His grace; He's showing them an enormous kindness. I have to admit that if God gave me these two options—be led by Moses and an angel or go with me and possibly have to kill me at some point—I'm not sure I'd struggle with it very long. What about you?

What were God's last words to them (Exodus 33:5c)?

_____.

What anxiety this had to have produced among them; we hate the unknown, especially when we are fully aware of what we deserve! The threat of losing God's presence sent the people of Israel into fear and mourning. I wonder . . . had God withdrawn His presence of the cloud by day and pillar of fire by night at this point? Just curious. That certainly would have helped Israel understand the significance of their immediate loss. And surely, they were affected by the fact that the tent in which Moses met with God was outside the camp. Every day as they witnessed God's presence coming down in a pillar of cloud to meet with Moses was a reminder that He was keeping His distance from them.

Again, Moses goes before God on Israel's behalf. Read the encounter in Exodus 33:12–17. What was Moses seeking?

_____.

Moses's plea is that God Himself and not an angel will not only lead them but also restore them into a relationship. I have heard many sermons on this section of scripture teaching that God answered Moses in verse 14 but Moses was so passionate about his cause that he didn't seem to notice. I am in no position to argue with that, nor would I even want to. But I can't help but notice something different than that here. Most translations show verses 14 and 15 as God saying, "My Presence will go with you," and "If your Presence does not go with me/us, do not send us up from here."

The *me* and *us* are not present in the original text, but we can easily see why they were translated this way from verse 16 as twice Moses stresses a distinction between himself and Israel ("me and your people"). It doesn't looks to me like Moses was doubting or questioning God's promise as some have suggested, nor was he overly excited and not listening. It appears to me that he wanted clarification on God's exact promise; Moses was looking for an "us"! I think he understood perfectly God's promise to go with him (verse 14), but he persevered until it included all of Israel.

What was God's reply to Moses's appeal (verse 17)?

_____

_____.

God calls Moses back up Mount Sinai. Read Exodus 34:1–7.
I intended to bring this up earlier and certainly don't want us to miss it. What does verse 5 in this chapter, as well as Exodus 19:18 and 20, say God has to do to reach Mount Sinai?

_____.

The visual pictured here is an excellent reminder that He is indeed Most High. Regardless of how elevated mankind may become, whether through technology, wealth, knowledge, or our own sense of self-importance, God still has to look down to see it, incline His ear to hear it or descend to deal with it. Just saying.

The text says God proclaimed Himself as compassionate and gracious, slow to anger, abounding in love (hesed) and faithfulness.

God has many attributes. Why do you suppose these are the particular ones He accentuates now?

_____

_____.

These specific traits that proclaim His name as the LORD are those that Moses and Israel have seen displayed since their exodus. Remember back in Exodus 6, God told Moses He would make Himself known by a name they were unfamiliar with. He accomplished that, and Israel now knows by experience a new side of Him.

God renews His covenant with Israel, replaces the broken tablets of the Ten Commandments, and work begins in the construction of the tabernacle. The final chapter of Exodus tells of the erection of the tabernacle with all its intricacies. In reading over the details once again, my heart was so moved when I got to verses 12–15.

Read them yourself (Exodus 40:12–15). How do these verses affect you? Explain:

_____

_____.

What a moment for God and Israel! It had been one year since these people left Egypt and nine months after their arrival at Sinai. They had both learned a lot about each other. The first year of marriage is never easy, is it? The final verses tell us Moses finished the work and the cloud of God's glory filled the tabernacle. Read Exodus 40:34–38. Did God fulfill His promise to be present with Israel?

_____

_____.

What had the people of Israel done that led to God's presence being manifested in such a powerful way (reference Exodus 39:42–43—I'm just looking for one word here)? They _____.

Obedience to God always brings about His blessings. God's glory can fall and fill us when we determine to live a life of obedience. Don't we want a life consumed with the fire of God's glory?

Moses is a forerunner of a mediator to come. God had placed and prepared Moses for this position of intercessor, and through it, He would reveal His heart of love and compassion for His people. I can't help but notice how often Moses's interaction with God resembles that of a loving spouse with their partner, specifically as it relates to their children.

Read the interaction in Exodus 33:12–17 and see if you would agree.
The progression of the mediation is noteworthy.

- Moses pleads with God not to destroy Israel, and then . . .
- Moses seeks forgiveness for Israel, and then . . .
- Moses seeks God's manifest presence for Israel.

Moses does not stop intervening for the Israelites until He has achieved for them everything God was willing to give. This serves as a very important lesson for us. Intercession is a critical role for believers.

What does Exodus 19:6 and Revelation 5:10 say God's people are?

_____ .

One of the major roles of a priest is to intercede on behalf of the people. Read Ezekiel 22:30. What does it tell us God looks for?

_____ .

Intercession is not to be viewed as a need to alter God's plans or purposes but to be so intimately involved with Him that we share His mind and purpose and seek it from Him.

Moses's prayers on behalf of Israel set a beautiful example for us in dealing with those in our lives who don't know God or are far from Him. In following that example, we can plead with God:

- That they not be counted with those prepared for destruction (Romans 9:22)
- Remind Him that it is not His desire that any should perish but that all should come to the saving knowledge of Christ (2 Peter 3:9)
- We can ask God to grant them repentance, leading them to a knowledge of the truth (2 Timothy 2:25).
- Remind Him that if He kept a record of wrongs, no one could stand, but with Him, there is forgiveness (Psalm 130:3).
- We can ask Him to give them His Spirit of wisdom and revelation so that they may know Him better; flood their hearts with light that they see the hope to which they are called (Ephesians 1:17–18).

If Moses's example is any indication, we can surely expect God to be pleased and say to us what He said to Moses: "I will do the very thing you have asked, because I am pleased with you and I know you by name."

Moses is an Israelite, just like the others, but his love and commitment to God set him apart. It is his example we aspire to, not to that of the harlot Israel. Moses's face-to-face knowledge of God created the intimate bond God desires with all His people. We'd be wise to evaluate our own relationship. Would it look like the one Moses had with God, or would it be more reflective of the Israelites? Without a God-given grasp of the nature of the amazing union we've been chosen to experience with Him, we will end up like the Israelites who, in a matter of days, forsook their Beloved for an idol.

God loves us like a parent loves a child—with nurture and affection. He loves us like a shepherd loves stupid, helpless sheep—with compassion and protection. He loves us like a treasured friend—with loyalty and commitment. His love encompasses all these things, and for the most part, they are areas we are familiar and comfortable with. But no matter how unfamiliar or uncomfortable it may be, we need to realize that He also loves us like a groom loves his bride—passionately, emotionally, longingly, protectively, faithfully, and jealously. This is a love to be cherished.

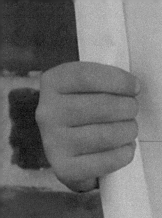

DAY 1

In spite of God's presence dwelling with Israel, they continued to struggle with obedience and trust. Their unbelief in God's promise and power kept them wandering in the wilderness rather than possessing the home God had given them. When they refused to believe God would defeat those occupying the land they were to have, it gave a wrong opinion of God to the surrounding nations. God's desire was to reveal Himself to them through Israel.

What was God's stated intent or purpose for Israel according to Exodus 34:10?

_____ .

God had given Israel His name. They received it, and it became their identity just as a bride takes the name of her husband, and the two are recognized as one. Israel's unbelief was a violation of their vow not to take God's name in vain.

Here's a simple analogy: Let's say you were a homeless, single mother of ten and Bill Gates comes along and marries you. Your identity would no longer be Jane Doe, destitute single mother, but Jane Doe Gates—wealthy wife of a very powerful man. As his name bearer, all of your needs would be met and then some. Therefore, it would be inconceivable that you would dress in rags, go without food, or continue to live on the street. If you did, you would have taken his name in vain; it would be for nothing when everything you needed was available through your identification with the name.

Israel bore witness of God to other nations; the nations knew God through Israel. How frustrating it must be to God when we refuse the power and sufficiency that comes from bearing His name. To not call upon and depend on His great name is to have received it in vain.

What explanation does Numbers 15:41 give for God bringing Israel out of Egypt?

_____.

What distinguishes Israel from other nations in Deuteronomy 4:7?

_____.

God brought Israel out for the purpose of intimacy. They were chosen to receive His name, be identified with Him and live with Him.

A new generation of Israel was raised up and would finally be able to possess the land God had promised hundreds of years ago. The entire book of Deuteronomy was written for them. Since they had not personally witnessed the exodus, the parting of the Red Sea, or the events at Mount Sinai, Deuteronomy is an explanation and reiteration of the law. It's written in similar form to a covenant treaty, composed of the preamble (Deuteronomy 1:1–5), historic prologue (Deuteronomy 1:6–4:49), requirements/obligations (Deuteronomy 5:1–26:19) and blessings and curses (Deuteronomy 27:1, 30:20).

Deuteronomy is considered the last will and testament of Moses. In his final words, we can almost hear the desperation as he pleads with Israel to love God, to obey Him, and to watch themselves carefully because their default mode was adultery. God loves Israel exclusively, and He expects the same from them.

What does Deuteronomy 4:24 say about Him?

_____.

What does Deuteronomy 6:1–3 and 10:12–13 cite as God's purpose for giving the law?

_____.

Chapter 6 of Deuteronomy, verses 4–5, is where the Shema comes from; the word means "hear." It's a declaration devote Jews recite every day, morning and evening. Read them now.

The very first word, _hear_, infers not just hearing but taking action with what's been heard. Just as saying to a child, "Did you hear what I said?" is not just asking if the words were heard but also why there's no action regarding those words. Grasping how to love God with all our heart, soul, and strength can be difficult. Loving Him with all our hearts is not complicated, but soul and strength is difficult to translate into action. I found a modern translation of the Shema really helpful:

> Listen up Israel, The Lord is your God, He, and He alone! You should love Him with every thought that you think, live every hour of every day for Him, be willing to sacrifice your life for Him. Love Him with every penny in your wallet and everything that you've got! (_Walking in the Dust of Rabbi Jesus_, Lois Tverberg)

35

This translation helps to clarify that God expects the love we have for Him to be all-consuming. It should affect every aspect of our being—our thoughts, time, money, our very lives. Nothing can be withheld. This love is not just something we feel; it's more importantly something we do. So I have two questions:

Why does He demand this extreme love commitment?

_____

_____

_____.

How are you doing with it? What area/areas are you falling short?

_____

_____

_____.

God does not need our love. He's fully satisfied in Himself; therefore, His command for us to love Him is not for His benefit but ours. Areas of inadequacy in our love for God must not be dismissed, because only when we love God with everything we are and have will we be safe from destructive affections. Obedience to God enables Him to pour out His blessings, while disobedience causes us to forfeit the safety, security and satisfaction that He gives.

Remembering to be obedient requires determination; without a concerted effort to follow God, we quickly begin to go our own way.

Moses goes through the terms of the covenant with Israel and recaps the blessings that will occur from obedience, as well as the curses that will fall on them from disobedience. These start in chapter 27 and are summed up very simply in Deuteronomy 30:15. Write it here:

_____.

Read all of chapter 30. What does Moses say about these commands in verse 11?

_____.

Verse 19 states a choice has been set before them—life and death or blessings and curses. What does He then instruct the people to do?

_____

What would you suspect his tone might be in this instruction?

_____

How does Moses further define *life* in Deuteronomy 30:20b and 32:47?

_____ .

Choosing God and His words is an exclusive selection not to be taken lightly. Loving them solely will bring about a blessed life. The choice is very simple but not easy, and we're all about easy. Conceptually, the choice is obvious; anyone would choose blessings over curses and life over death. It's the fleshing it out that trips us up and finds us living contrary to our own convictions.

Based on Moses's experience with this group's predecessors, what would you suspect Moses's approach to them would be in delivering these final words?

_____ .

Moses's words were strong and to the point. How do you suppose Israel received these challenging directives? Would they listen to Moses? Why or why not?

_____
_____
_____ .

What a man Moses was! He displayed faithful, wholehearted love for his God. He was an excellent example of strong leadership, demonstrating mercy, compassion, and great love for the people he led. A number of other men have received great acclaim from the Lord: Enoch walked with God. David was a man after God's own heart. John was the disciple Jesus loved. But no other man was given the designation as someone God knew face-to-face.

Read Deuteronomy 34:1–5.

Tears are welling up in my eyes as I read this. How about you? It's really difficult to articulate why I would be sorrowful; there's just something so beautiful about a life so well lived that it has to be mourned, from this perspective anyway. On the other hand, I believe that God was waiting in great anticipation of this homecoming.

What does Psalm 116:15 say?

_____ .

I see God flinging open the gates of heaven to hurry out to welcome His faithful servant. There would be no awkwardness at this encounter (if that ever happens at all) because these two already knew each other very well.

Moses's final words were a pronouncement of blessings on the Israelites, and like a great coach about to send his team back out on the field, he gives an amazing speech.

Read it in Deuteronomy 33:26–29, and as you read, do it with the view of God as Israel's loving and faithful husband. Read it slowly and allow it to create pictures in your mind.

"Blessed are you, O Israel! Who is like you, a people saved by the Lord? He is your shield and helper and your glorious sword"

DAY 2

God remained faithful to his covenant promises by, under Joshua's leadership, bringing Israel into the land He had vowed to give them. Read Joshua 21:43–45 and write verse 45.

_____.

We see God's grace, His undeserved favor, displayed as Israel possessed the land. Read Joshua 24:11–13 and state all of the things God did for them.

_____
_____
_____.

Look at all God did for them, and they did not have to raise a finger—that's grace! Joshua had been a great leader to Israel; he stayed true to God and showed great faith (crossing the flooded Jordan, circumcising the men on the front lines of Jericho, marching around Jericho until the walls fell). Joshua's farewell address to the people contain the famous words familiar to almost everyone. Write them here (Joshua 24:15a and d):

_____
_____
_____.

Like Moses, Joshua wanted to remind Israel there is a choice that must be made. They would serve the one true God or some other, but they couldn't do both.

The end of Joshua's leadership brought in a turbulent time for Israel known as the period of the judges. This phase in Israel's history is summed up in Judges 17:6 and 21:25; what does it say?

_____.

Israel had a king—the King of kings. He was their ruler, guide, and sovereign. But they didn't function very well without a godly human leader. Israel demanded a king to rule over them, but their purpose for insisting was not to help their waywardness. What was the reason they give in 1 Samuel 8:20 for wanting a king?

_____.

God had called this ragamuffin bunch out for the purpose of setting them apart; the fact that they were different was the point! But this crew wants to look like everyone else. It appears that what they really wanted was a person they could show off, a powerful warrior who could lead their army and impress the other nations. It was all about image.

Doesn't this sound similar to the people's words in Exodus 32:1? They desired something/someone they could see to flaunt and boast about. What a horrible and blatant affront to God. How does Psalm 47:2 describe God the King?

_____.

What does Psalm 60:11–12 say about a human king?

_____.

Psalm 93:1a states the Lord is robed in _____ and armed with _____.

Who does the very first line of Psalm 24:8 declare Him to be?

_____.

Psalm 2:2–4 asserts that kings and rulers of the earth gather together to oppose and plot against God. How is God identified?

_____.

What is His reaction to this plot?

_____.

Okay, so why does Israel want a king? Can you say *rock head*? No, I believe the correct biblical term is *stiff-necked*. All kidding aside, Israel is not rejecting an arbitrary leader; they're rejecting their partner. The one robed in splendor, who strides forward in the greatness of His strength, who is mighty to save (Isaiah 63:1)…is Israel's husband.

What is God's reply to this outrageous demand (1 Samuel 8:22)?

_____.

The worst thing that can ever happen is for God to give us the demands of our twisted and prideful desires. God does indeed give Israel a king—King Saul. You probably recall how that worked out for them. Then God showed His enduring love by graciously anointing a king who, like Moses, would be a representation of someone to come. King David was a godly leader for Israel, and God would use his throne to establish His eternal kingdom. He employed King David's son Solomon to build a temple in Jerusalem in which His name would dwell. In spite of the fact that Solomon's temple was massive, exquisite, and extravagant, he seemed overwhelmed at the thought of God dwelling there.

What does Solomon say in 2 Chronicle 6:18 that express His incredulity?

_____.

Read 2 Chronicles 7:1–3. What happened when Solomon finished praying?

_____

_____.

This is just like the account we studied in Exodus 40 when the work on the tabernacle was complete. The pattern is clear: _God fills the place in which His Name dwells_. Israel will prove incapable of being faithful to her Husband. She will openly display her desire for other gods throughout the Old Testament. Any other husband would have kicked her to the curb by now.

What does 2 Timothy 2:13 say about God?

_____.

Let's look at just a few of the Old Testament examples of God's pursuit of the harlot, Israel. At God's instruction, Elijah confronts Israel with their flagrant Baal worship in 1 Kings 18. He poses a question to all of Israel (18:21). What was it?

_____.

How do the people respond?

_____.

Whether you know the story or not, read the account in 1 Kings 18:22–40. What are the most striking things for you in this depiction?

_____ .

What a truly awesome display of power! Why would God prove Himself this way to this adulterous group?

_____ .

God desires for her to return; He wants her back. Amazing! I don't understand the depths of God's love for His people, nor do I understand the superficial love of Israel (and very often my own).

The entire book of Isaiah pictures Israel's unfaithfulness and God's redeeming love. This book has sixty-six chapters; the Bible has sixty-six books. The first thirty-nine chapters deal with judgment/denunciation as do the thirty-nine books of the Old Testament. The remaining twenty-seven chapters are about consolation/restoration, just as the twenty-seven books for the New Testament are. (That is *very* cool!) Read Isaiah 1:2–4 and sum up the problem as God portrays it:

_____

_____

_____ .

What does God call Israel in Isaiah 1:21?

_____ .

The parable of the vineyard in Isaiah 5 describes God's experience with Israel. Read Isaiah 5:1–7.
Note Isaiah's choice of opening words: "I will sing for the one I love a song about his vineyard." God is the one he loves, so possibly, Isaiah was identifying himself as the friend of the bridegroom. This love song figuratively depicts the bride and groom as the vineyard and its owner. This is a love song about God and Israel.

Israel is depicted as the vineyard. What specifically had God done for the vineyard (verse 5:2)?

_____ .

In spite of all that, what did the vineyard produce (verse 2c and 4b)?

_____ .

God tells Israel to make a judgment between the two (He and the vineyard). Who is at fault? Could He / should He have done more than He did? It's a rhetorical question because what legitimate response could they possibly have?

The first thirty-nine chapters of Isaiah prophesy of God's coming judgment; God's people will be taken captive by the Babylonians. The Babylonians were brutal in the siege of Jerusalem. You can read about it in Jeremiah 52. Write Jeremiah 52:3:

_____

_____.

Despite all the horror that will come upon God's people, chapters 40 and on in Isaiah describe the hope He extends. Write the opening words God dictates to Isaiah 40:1–2:

_____

_____

_____.

After revealing the harsh reality that was about to come upon this people because of their sin, these words of hope were like a lifeline. God would not completely forsake them; He calls them "my people" and Himself "your God." This is covenant language; He's reminding them of His hesed.

Read Isaiah 54:5–8. God reminds Israel that He is her _____.

Verse 6 says He will _____ as if she were a _____.

DAY 3

Like Isaiah, Prophet Ezekiel uses parables to illustrate Israel's gross sin, comparing her to an adulterous woman in chapter 16 and two harlots (Israel and Judah) in chapter 23. Both are excellent illustrations for our context, but I have to tell you, the parable of the two sisters is so very graphic and candid that I could not think of an appropriate way to study it together; it's quite embarrassing! (Are you all racing to that chapter now?) But in spite of all its explicit awkwardness, it really should be studied as it reveals the true nature of how God views the affections and loyalties we develop apart from Him. Maybe you can do that on your own.

We'll just stick with chapter 16. John MacArthur describes this chapter in his commentary as "so sad and indicting that some of the ancient rabbis did not allow it to be read in public." Read Ezekiel 16:1–43; it's a lot, but that's why we're here, right?

The chapter begins with Israel's infancy. She is described as unwanted and uncared for; she was thrown out and left to die from exposure. What did God do for her (verse 6–7)?

_____.

This probably refers to Israel's development during the 430 years in Egypt.

Verse 8 says Israel was _____. This means she was of a marriageable age. Spreading His garment over her was to claim her in marriage (Ruth 3:9). These scriptures confirm the concept that God entered into a covenant of marriage with Israel. The verses go on to tell of the wedding gifts she received that were indicative of a queen. She was washed (mikveh) by God; her cleansing and consecration was His work.

How is she described in verses 13c and 14?

_____.

How did she get this designation (verse 14)?

_____.

What happens next (verse 15)?

_____.

From verse 14 through 42 the word *prostitute* or *prostitution* is used thirteen times! The Bible is not known to exaggerate a point; if anything, it's considerably understated. Ezekiel is not trying to make a point. It's made; he's just hammering away at it. I find verse 32 to be heart-wrenching. Write it here:

_____.

What is God's emotion regarding Israel as stated in Ezekiel 6:9?

_____.

What will God do according to Ezekiel 16:60?

_____.

God's plan to betroth His people to Himself will not be thwarted. The marriage picture that began in the garden and became more pronounced at Sinai now promises to develop more clearly in the future with God's promise of an everlasting covenant.

The book of Hosea was written to express God's steadfast love for Israel in spite of her continued unfaithfulness depicted by Hosea the prophet's marital experience.

Read Hosea 1:1–3. What does the Lord call Hosea to do?

_____.

What reason does He give for asking this?

_____.

There seems to be a fair amount of controversy among scholars whether or not Gomer was a prostitute before Hosea married her or if she became unfaithful afterward. Some commentators state Gomer's adultery is to be understood proleptically (meaning, it's anticipated, a future event). Gomer will prove to be unfaithful. The first and most compelling reasoning behind this thought is this union was to reflect Israel's marriage to God, and when God betrothed her at Sinai, she was not promiscuous. Secondly, why would she be rebuked and rejected because of her prostitution when she was a known prostitute? And finally, a prophet marrying a known prostitute brings up an issue of ethics.

In contrast, others believe Gomer was a known prostitute at the time of her marriage. They cite the fact that God often asked His prophets to do strange things, so this request would not be unusual. In addition, because Israel (mankind) has been a self-seeking sinful people from the very beginning, Gomer, as the image of Israel, would understandably be promiscuous.

What do you think? Based on these arguments, what would be your reason for your opinion?

_____

_____.

Whatever your conclusion, it's advantageous to think it through, examine the evidence, and come up with your own opinion based on the information. Reliable commentaries are a valuable Bible study tool, but their purpose is to assist us in coming to our own conclusions rather than mechanically accepting theirs.

Hosea and Gomer have three children, each with a symbolic name. What are they?
(If your Bible does not provide the meaning, blueletterbible.com is a good resource.)
Jezreel means _____ (Hosea 1:4).
Lo-Ruhamah means _____ (Hosea 1:6).
Lo-Ammi means _____ (Hosea 1:9).

The children symbolized the coming judgment on Israel when they would be scattered in exile to the Assyrians along with the removal of His favor.

Gomer apparently left Hosea after the birth of their third child and began to prostitute herself. In spite of that, what is the Lord's instruction to Hosea in Hosea 3:1?

_____.

Hosea is told to love her as _____.

What does Gomer/Israel attribute to her lovers (2:5b)?

_____.

Because she didn't acknowledge that all her blessings came from God, He would take them all away. Verse 3b says, "I will make her like a desert, turn her into a parched land, and slay her with thirst." Spiritually speaking, what do you understand that to mean?

_____.

DAY 4

Where does the Lord say He will lead Israel (Hosea 2:14b)?

_____.

    The desert is a place, physically and symbolically, often used by the Lord. Whether His purpose is to discipline willful sin or to develop a mature faith, the desert is always a testing ground.
    Read Deuteronomy 8:2–5. Why does the text say God led Israel into the desert?

_____.

    From Deuteronomy 8:3, insert the word your Bible uses: "He humbled you,

_____ you hunger."

    Whatever word your translation uses, the lesson in the desert is the same; God causes/allows/lets His people experience hardship for the purpose of finding Him sufficient to fill the need. We are usually brought into the leanness of a desert experience from a time of abundance, whether tangible or spiritual. You may or may not be unaware that although the Israelites were slaves in Egypt, the land was lush and beautiful; it was a rich source of vegetables, grains, and fish. For four hundred years, this was the land they were accustomed to; they had no skills for operating in the harsh and extreme conditions of the desert. Ill-equipped and unfamiliar was purposeful; the Lord led His people into the desert to grow their faith.
    Similarly, the people whom Hosea prophesied to were living during a time of rich material prosperity, both economically and agriculturally, which led to moral corruption as they attributed their prosperity to other gods.

    Hosea 2:7b states God's reason for Israel's coming desert experience. What is His purpose?

_____.

    What word does Hosea 2:14 use to describe how God will get Israel to the desert? He will

_____ her.

"The word *allure* connotes persuasion by means of attractive benefits" (NIV Bible Commentary). The desert, along with every other activity of God in our lives, is for our benefit . . . always.

The book of Hosea goes on to give an indictment of Israel; the Lord brings charges against her. According to Hosea 4:1, what are the charges?

_____.

Hosea 4:6a reveals the reason for Israel's destruction. What is it?

_____.

A deficiency in our knowledge of God and His Word will always be destructive: "A people without understanding will come to ruin!" (Hosea 4:14c).
Read the following verses and match them with their meaning.

1. Psalm 111:10 — Understanding God's statutes brings life.

2. Psalm 119:130 — From God's mouth comes knowledge and understanding.

3. Psalm 119:144 — Knowledge comes from fearing the Lord.

4. Proverbs 1:7 — Trust God, not your own understanding.

5. Proverbs 2:6 — Following God's precepts bring understanding.

6. Proverbs 3:5 — The unfolding of God's Word gives understanding, even to the simple.

What insight do these scriptures give regarding what kind of knowledge and understanding is needed?

_____
_____.

Israel's downfall has always been their deficient understanding of the intimate relationship God desired with them and offered to them. They were invited to know Him beyond facts and information; they could know Him like a wife knows a husband. But their corrupt hearts would not (could not?) be faithful to only one God. They didn't seem to be able to understand the exclusivity of the relationship; they appeared to think they could have this God along with many others. In spite of the strong words used to describe Israel (harlot, prostitute, whore), they either didn't understand the gravity of their unfaithfulness—that it was adultery—or they just didn't care. It's hard to say.

Day 5

How does Hosea 6:4 describe Israel's love for God?

_____.

It's worthy of note that He doesn't say they have no love for Him. He says it's fleeting; it doesn't last. Israel obeyed the letter of the law; they followed the sacrificial system, honored the Sabbath, celebrated the feasts, etc., but they included ritual worship of other gods. They relied on foreign alliances for protection and trusted in their prosperity to sustain them.

Israel never overtly rejected God; they just refused to acknowledge that their fickle love and commitment to Him was a rejection. Because of it, the hammer was about to fall.

The Lord reminds them in Hosea 6:6a what He desires instead of sacrifice. What is it?

_____.

It's been a while, but any guesses what the original Hebrew word for this is?

_____.

Verse 6b states another quality God seeks ahead of burnt offerings. What is it?

_____.

God sought from Israel faithful, steadfast, loyal love (hesed), and an intimate knowledge of Him. The statement did not negate what they were commanded to do; obedience is crucial, and God had commanded that they offer sacrifices and burnt offerings. But rote obedience is not enough. In fact, scripture indicates it's unacceptable (Isaiah 1:11–17, Amos 5:21–24, Micah 6:6–8). Israel obeyed the letter of the law but missed the spirit of it, which was to offer themselves.

Read Isaiah 29:13. What are the people accused of?

_____

_____.

What was missing in their worship?

_____
_____.

Obedience must be accompanied by genuine love for God and a desire to please Him. He's looking for true faith, not empty sacrifice. God's judgments will in fact descend on Israel: Ephraim will be _____ (Hosea 5:9). I will _____ on them like a flood of water (Hosea 5:10b). For I will be like a lion to Ephraim, like a great lion to Judah. I will _____ and go away; I will _____, with no one to rescue them (Hosea 5:14).

What do verses 7:13 and 11:5–6 say is the reason destruction is coming on them?

_____
_____.

Hosea 11:2a says, "But the more I called Israel, the further they went from me." I think the most immediate image from this verse for most of us is of an obstinate child in that terrifying moment when you're shouting at them to come to you as they run toward a busy street. That would certainly be an accurate description of God's people. However, in the context of Hosea's depiction of Israel as an adulterous wife, the sentiment goes from alarming to heartbreaking.

Read Hosea 11:3–4. Count how many times the pronoun *I* is used: _____

What are the things God said He did for Ephraim (Israel)?

_____
_____
_____.

God personally took on all the responsibility of Israel's development. The above verses reveal God's patience, mercy, commitment, deliverance, and provision for Israel. How apropos is God's question we looked at early in Isaiah 5:4: "What more was there to do for my vineyard [my people], that I have not done in it?"

Ezekiel was given a vision in chapters 8–11 of the progressive departure of God's glory from Jerusalem. Because of the extreme moral and spiritual corruption of the nation's leadership, God would bring judgment on Jerusalem.

In the temple, God's glory resided in the most holy place between the wings of the cherubs which were on each side of the ark of the covenant over the mercy seat. His glory now moves to the threshold or door of the temple (Ezekiel 10:4), then to the east gate (10:18–19), and finally to the mountain east of the temple, which is the Mount of Olives (11:22–23). God has removed His presence, His face, from Israel.

If ever there was to be a people who loved God passionately, faithfully, with all their heart, soul and strength, it should have been Israel. But like Adam and Eve, a perfect love for God fleshed out through obedience was impossible for Israel's corrupted hearts. God's longing for a bride appears unattainable.

The canvas displaying the first strokes of the brush in its beautiful picture of marriage, beginning in Eden and gaining more definition at Sinai, is left unfinished. Although there were times the brush was poised in anticipation, as the prophets foretold what was hoped to be an imminent restoration, the brush remains idle, and the canvas displays only shadows.

Well, it was a really heroic try on God's part. Too bad, it didn't work out. The good news is He's a triune God, so at least they still have each other. This describes the deserved ending, but Scripture reveals that God *will* have a bride—a holy, beautiful bride that loves Him as He loves her.

Hosea 2:16 speaks of a coming day when God's people will no longer call Him "my master" but "my _____."

God was not satisfied with a relationship with His people that was based on fear and focused only on obedience. He very much anticipated a marriage-like relationship founded on love and commitment. He desired His people to consider Him their husband rather than their master.

Israel will no longer be called deserted or desolate but declared Hephzibah, meaning "my delight," and Beulah, which means "married," and God will rejoice over His bride (Isaiah 62:4 and 5b). God's people knew the despair that comes from being forsaken and left desolate, deprived of God's presence. These verses hold forth the hope and confident expectation that God will once again delight in her and enjoy the oneness and love that the image of marriage promises.

Read what the Lord's plans are in Hosea 2:19–20 and write this amazing and beautiful promise here:

_____

_____

_____

John MacArthur explains these scriptures well in his commentary: *I will betroth you.* "Repeated three times, the term emphasizes the intensity of God's restoring love for the nation. In that day, Israel will no longer be thought of as a prostitute. Israel brings nothing to the marriage; God makes all the promises and provides all the dowry. These verses are recited by every orthodox Jew as he places the phylacteries on his hand and forehead (cf. Deut. 11:18)."

We can see from Isaiah 59:16 that the Lord will take it on Himself to change the condition of His people. Write the verse here:

_____

_____

_____.

Why is all this important? Why have we spent an entire week on adulterous Israel? Because Israel serves as an example to us. We need to learn from their lives. As the saying goes, people who don't learn from history are destined to repeat it. Israel's problem was they didn't love God exclusively. They would not learn that He was more than enough, and they didn't need other lovers. The purpose of this study is to reveal the amazing steadfast love God has for His people so that we might respond to it and not repeat the error. I wish I had more admirable words; I wish I could expound with eloquence to help achieve a true understanding of His love, but I can't. Nevertheless, even now, I am praying that God will enlighten the eyes of your heart so that you may be able to grasp how wide and long and high and deep His love is for you personally.

God loves His people powerfully . . . faithfully . . . unconditionally. We've grown so accustomed to hearing this that I fear it fails to appropriately compute. This should not be; His love is truly inconceivable! We should be moved to marvel at the depths of it, be amazed, in awe; it surpasses knowledge (Ephesians 3:19).

Does the fact that God's love surpasses knowledge cause you to be in awe? Does it inspire wonder and amazement, or do you mentally write it off as unattainable and move on?

_____

_____

_____.

If your honest attitude toward God's love is apathetic or half-hearted please don't disregard or deny it; it's too important. I have felt guilty in the past, knowing that I did not love the Lord with all my heart, soul, and strength, but pushed it aside because I didn't really know what that even meant, much less what I could do about it. How could I make myself love God? I didn't understand that my heart is His work. Confessing the deficiency, I asked Him to rectify it.

Deuteronomy 30:6 is God's Word on the subject and serves as a perfect prayer for an indifferent heart. Write it here:

_____

_____

_____.

David, the man after God's own heart, had a request from God that we would do well to duplicate. Write it here (Psalm 51:10a):

_____

_____ .

God can and will empower you to love Him, as well as enable you to grasp His deep love for you. Understanding God's profound love makes it possible to walk in obedience to His Word with a sincere desire to please him rather than fear of displeasing Him. It's good to fear the Lord, but fear is not our motivation. Love is the motivation.

God's glory has departed from Israel and Malachi, the last of the prophets, has spoken the Lord's final words to the people. God was silent for four hundred years, but not idle.

Read Isaiah 43:18–19 then write it here: _____

_____

_____ .

Stay tuned, and we'll discover what God was up to, what took Him four hundred years to do! I'll leave you with a superb description of hesed—the steadfast, loyal love God displays:

> The word hesed . . . [is] the descriptor par excellence of God in the Old Testament. The word speaks of a completely undeserved kindness and generosity done by a person who is in a position of power. This was the Israelites' experience of God. He revealed himself to them when they were not looking for him, and he kept his covenant with them long after their persistent breaking of it had destroyed any reason for his continued keeping of it. . . . Unlike humans, this deity was not fickle, undependable, self-serving, and grasping. Instead he was faithful, true, upright, and generous—always. (*The Bible among the Myths*, John Oswalt)

Jesus: Covenant Keeper and Bridegroom

Follow Up to Introduction

The Bible is not just a documentation of historical facts but the record of God fulfilling His Word. If we don't know that yet, we will definitely know it by the end of this study! Following this thread of God's desire for a people, a bride, has illuminated the most beautiful pictures of His amazing plan, revealing His intent and design in fulfilling it.

As promised from our first lesson, we will reexamine both the covenant God made with His people and the elements of a Jewish wedding. We'll see how transferring from old covenant to new will usher in the bride of Christ and Jesus's role in fulfilling them as both Covenant Keeper and Bridegroom.

If you recall, God cut a unilateral covenant with Abraham—meaning, He (God) took responsibility for both parties. The smoking fire pot (smoke) and blazing torch (fire) were both representative of God. In that, there was never any confusion of what the outcome would be in binding Himself to His people through covenant. Your homework last week exposed the miserable failure of God's people in keeping the old covenant which, according to the stipulations, would cost the life of the covenant breaker.

The problem with the first covenant was sin. God's covenant required obedience in order to receive His blessings. Israel continually failed to keep God's law, thus breaking the covenant. God, however, would be faithful to His promises; He would not break the covenant but would initiate the means to achieve its fulfillment. God's original purpose to "take" a people (Israel, His firstborn son) to Himself would come to fruition through His one and only Son Jesus.

The genealogy in Matthew and Luke point out three important identities of Christ: Jesus is the new Adam, the new David, and the new Israel. We will only examine Jesus as the new Adam and Israel as these have a direct association with our subject.

First, Jesus is the new (or "last") Adam. Luke's genealogy of Jesus takes His lineage back to Adam. Romans tell us that Adam was a type of pattern of One to come (Romans 5:14). The first Adam brought sin and death to all mankind. Jesus, the "last Adam" (1 Corinthians 15:45), brings life and forgiveness of sin to all that come to Him.

Luke ends Jesus's genealogy by saying, "The son of Adam, the son of God" (Luke 3:37d). Just as Adam's birth was supernatural, so too Jesus. The Son of God, the Word that was with God and was God, became flesh. God became a man in every physical sense of the word. Therefore, because

God's people will find it completely impossible to fulfill their covenant with Him, Jesus—sinless, perfect God wrapped in human flesh (somehow!)—will take on the costly role of Covenant Keeper.

Secondly, Jesus is the new Israel. Matthew 1:1 states, "A record of the genealogy of Jesus Christ the son of David, the son of Abraham." Per God's covenant promise, Abraham's seed will become the great nation of Israel. In his book *Is Jesus in the Old Testament?* Iain Duguid states this genealogy identifies Jesus as the true Son of Abraham and, therefore, the true Israel. Not only that, he goes on to show how Matthew describes Jesus's personal reenactment of Israel's history. Let's look at that:

- Joseph (Jacob's son) goes to Egypt bringing about the establishment of the nation of Israel (Exodus 5:1–5). A man named Joseph brings his wife and young son, Jesus, to Egypt (Matthew 2:13–15).
- Israel escapes the loss of their firstborn sons—the first Passover (Exodus 12:21–23). After His birth, Jesus, God's firstborn son (Hebrew 1:6a), escapes Herod's plot to kill Him (Matthew 2:13–15).
- The prophet Hosea, speaking both historically and prophetically, says, "Out of Egypt I called my son" (Hosea 11:1). Israel is called God's firstborn son (Exodus 4:22) whom He brings out of Egypt. God calls His one and only Son out of Egypt (Matthew 2:19–20).
- Israel escaped certain death by passing through the waters of the Red Sea and emerged as a new nation on the other side. The waters of the Red Sea symbolized salvation. Israel was saved by God's power and gracious provision—as well as judgment—the Egyptian army was destroyed. Jesus submits to water baptism, which signified salvation by a symbolic death and resurrection (Romans 6:4). His baptism was a way of identifying Himself with us; it was not a confession of His own sin but ours. It also foreshadowed a future baptism He would undertake (Luke 12:50) to bear the weight of the sins of mankind that would bring about an "exodus," salvation for His people but judgment for those not identified with Him.
- Israel and Jesus were both tested in the wilderness—Israel for forty years, Jesus for forty days.

  1. They both became hungry. The Israelites grumbled against God because there was no bread (Exodus 16:2–3, 7). Jesus trusted God for His provisions and did not sin as Satan tempted Him to command stones to become bread. In His temptation, Jesus quotes Deuteronomy 8:3, the passage describing Israel's same test, saying, "Man does not live on bread alone but on every word that comes from the mouth of the Lord."
  2. Both Israel and Jesus were led to question God's presence. At Massah, Israel grumbled again against the Lord when there was no water, doubting that the Lord was with them. Moses responded to them, saying, "Why do you put the Lord to the test?" (Exodus 17:1–2). Satan tempted Jesus to throw Himself from the temple in order to prove God's presence. Jesus refused and quoted Deuteronomy 6:16, saying, "Do not test the Lord your God . . . as you did at Massah."

3. Both were tempted to worship other gods. Israel's appalling creation of the golden calf was the beginning of their continual worship of other gods, which incited Moses's appeal. Satan offered Jesus all the kingdoms of the world if He would worship him. Jesus again quotes Moses in his appeal to the Israelites to forsake other gods (Deuteronomy 6:13), saying, "Away from me, Satan! For it is written: Worship the Lord your God, and serve him only."

Israel and Jesus each faced three similar tests in their wildernesses. Israel failed every time, but Jesus flawlessly succeeded in each one. Duguid says, "Jesus was personally reenacting the history of Israel, only in reverse, succeeding where Israel had failed."

As the new Israel with whom the covenant was made, Jesus is the Covenant Keeper. Born—under the law, His faultless life of obedience fulfilled the law's demands, qualifying Him as the sacrificial lamb—perfect, without blemish as the law demanded. "The Lamb of God who takes away the sin of the world" (John 1:29).

The enormous outstanding debt for man's unfaithfulness demanded payment. The covenant was binding, cut in blood and broken by man; therefore, the blood of man would have to be spilled.

The dual representation of God walking the blood path foretold the humanity that He would assume to receive the just judgment for violating the covenant.

The outcome of the covenant God cut with Abraham would mean that Jesus, the fullness of God in bodily form (Colossians 2:9), the very nature of God made in human likeness (Philippians 2:6a and 7b), would take on the terrible punishment for man's failure and sin. The magnitude of this judgment is incomprehensible.

At this point, we need to transition (admittedly a bit awkwardly!) and return to the elements of a Jewish wedding as these two subjects now collide to reveal the almost completed picture of Jesus and His bride.

Above, Jesus is established as the Covenant Keeper. Now I will reiterate the points from the study's introduction and use Scripture to attest to Jesus's fulfillment as the Bridegroom:

Jesus came into the world to receive the bride of His Father's choosing:

- "For God so loved the world that He gave His one and only Son that whoever believes in Him shall not perish but have eternal life" (John 3:16).
- "To this John replied, 'A man can receive only what is given him from heaven. The bride belongs to the bridegroom'" (John 3:27 and 29a).
- "No one can come to me unless the Father who sent me draws him" (John 6:44a).

The ketubah, or marriage contract, is expressed in the new covenant. If you remember, the ketubah was essentially a statement of the husband's obligations; the wife's obligations were not recorded.

- "I will put my laws in their minds and write them on their hearts. I will be their God, and they will be my people. No longer will a man teach his neighbor, or a man his brother, saying, 'Know the Lord,' because they will all know me, from the least of them to the greatest. For I will forgive their wickedness and will remember their sins no more" (Hebrews 8:10b–12).

Paul, in Romans, uses wedding analogy to explain who we are bound to:

- "By law a married woman is bound to her husband as long as he is alive, but if her husband dies, she is released from the law of marriage. So, my brothers, you also died to the law through the body of Christ, that you might belong to another, to him who was raised from the dead, in order that we might bear fruit to God" (Romans 7:2 and 4).

The law has passed away; we are no longer bound to that but to Christ.

The bride price is determined. This is where our two subjects come together. As both Bridegroom and the one responsible for the broken covenant, this bride will cost Jesus everything.

Remember, the bride price was always and intentionally set high. I'm comfortable saying that Satan himself set the price of Jesus's bride as he was our master; it was his kingdom in which we resided. This bride price had to be negotiated, and if it were massive riches he had demanded, that would not have been a problem—God own the cattle on a thousand hills. However,

- "For you know that it was not with perishable things such as silver or gold that you were redeemed from the empty way of life handed down to you from your forefathers, but with the precious blood of Christ, a lamb without blemish or defect" (1 Peter 1:18–19).

We can see the enormous value placed on her in Jesus's reaction, which is grave:

- "Father, if you are willing, take this cup from me" (Luke 22:42a). This was not just any cup. Isaiah 51:17b and 22c and Jeremiah 25:15 describe it as the cup of God's wrath. We cannot even begin to understand what that means—God's wrath. It's *this* cup He seeks to avoid. Jesus had a thorough grasp of its terrifying implications. If He lifted this bitter cup to His lips, God's wrath would be poured out on Him in all its fullness and fury, and He know this.

As we discussed previously, many bridegrooms questioned the steep price that had been set for their bride. It would not have been unusual for the bridegroom to seek his father's advice as to the wisdom of the amount to be paid.

- "And being in anguish, he prayed more earnestly, and his sweat was like drops of blood falling to the ground" (Luke 22:44).

If that is what we are seeing from these scriptures, then I think we can also see the Father's response to Jesus:

- "An angel from heaven appeared to him and strengthened him" (Luke 22:43).

Jesus trusts His Father's judgment, saying:

- "Yet not my will, but yours be done" (Luke 22:42b).

The couple would share a cup of wine sealing the agreement. Partaking expressed the bridegroom's willingness to pay the bride price. Although Jesus understood the magnitude of drinking this cup, it would not pass from Him. Picture if you will—Jesus holding the cup at the last supper, peering into its crimson content, the color illustrative of the enormous sacrifice required was certainly not lost on Him. He perhaps swirled it around, contemplating all that this cup represents; it's not one to drink lightly, carelessly, or flippantly. One sip and His fate is sealed. But He raises the cup, presses it to His mouth, and drinks.

- "Then he took the cup, gave thanks and offered it to them, saying, 'Drink from it, all of you. This is my blood of the covenant, which is poured out for many for the forgiveness of sins'" (Matthew 26:27–28).

Shortly after, we begin to see God's wrath unleashed on the one and only Son of God, the Darling of Heaven.

As you read these scriptures, try to picture the scene—not to incite emotion but to understand/perceive the enormous price Jesus will pay for His bride, for you!

God's wrath begins to be unleashed, and it looks to me like it's almost progressive:

- "The men who were guarding Jesus began mocking and beating him. They blindfolded him and demanded, 'Prophesy! Who hit you?'" (Luke 22:63–64)
- "Then they spit in his face and struck him with their fists. Others slapped him" (Matthew 26:67).
- "Then Herod and his soldiers ridiculed and mocked him" (Luke 23:11a).
- Pilate "had Jesus flogged, and handed him over to be crucified. They stripped him and put a scarlet rob on him, and then twisted together a crown of thorns and set it on his head. They put a staff in his right hand and knelt in front of him and mocked him. 'Hail, king of the Jews!' they said. They spit on him, and took the staff and struck him on the head again and again. After they had mocked him, they took off the robe and put his own clothes on him. Then they led him away to crucify him" (Matthew 27:26, 28–31).
- "There were many who were appalled at him—his appearance was so disfigured beyond that of any man and his form marred beyond human likeness" (Isaiah 52:14).

Have you ever wondered why Jesus was tortured so much? Why couldn't He have just gone to the cross which was horrible enough? Jesus had to endure God's wrath on sin, and Jesus represented the full sin of mankind. Scripture states that He bore our sins in His body (1 Peter 2:24).

Jesus says, "Where I am going you cannot come" (John 13:33). Consider the weight of those words; let them fall all over you! You and I will *never* "go" where He went; we will *never* know the horror of God's wrath. We may suffer, but it won't be this! And we will *never* suffer to any extent with God's back to us, forsaken, as Christ was.

- "Carrying his own cross, he went out to the place of the Skull [which in Aramaic is called Golgotha]. Here they crucified him" (John 19:17–18a).
- "Jesus said, 'It is finished.' With that, he bowed his head and gave up his spirit" (John 19:30).

As God's acceptable representative for man, Jesus, the second Adam, the one who was without sin, drank the cup of God's wrath, sealing the covenant so that every person He represents would be guaranteed the lasting, unbreakable relationship with God that the new covenant offers.

The blood of Christ was spilled from the cross onto ground that was not far from the very ground on which the covenant was cut with Abraham. God keeps His Word. The Lord permanently attached His name to His covenant people at Mount Sinai and was willing to do whatever necessary to achieve His goal of having a holy people for Himself, a bride.

The bride shares the cup, expressing her willingness to enter into marriage. As with any proposal of marriage, the bride has to say yes—yes to Christ, yes to His free gift of salvation, yes to His imputed righteousness, yes to taking up the cross and following Him:

- "This cup is the new covenant in my blood; do this, whenever you drink it, in remembrance of me" (1 Corinthians 11:25b). We drink the cup to remember. We remember God's enormous love for us and the sacrifice required to redeem us, and it's to remember our own commitment to this covenant.

Preparation for the betrothal period included the mikveh, or spiritual cleaning. This cleansing was for both the bride and the groom.

- "In bringing many sons to glory, it was fitting that God, for whom and through whom everything exists, should make the author of their salvation perfect through suffering" (Hebrews 2:10).
- "And, once made perfect, he became the source of eternal salvation for all who obey him" (Hebrews 5:9).
- "Because by one sacrifice he has made perfect forever those who are being made holy" (Hebrews 10:14).

- "Just as Christ loved the church and gave himself up for her to make her holy, cleansing her by the washing with water through the word, and to present her to himself as a radiant church, without stain or wrinkle or any other blemish, but holy and blameless" (Ephesians 5:25b-27).

The couple comes together under the chuppah or covering:
- "Blessed are they whose transgressions are forgiven, whose sins are covered" (Romans 4:7).
- "Love covers over a multitude of sins" (1 Peter 4:8).

The bridegroom leaves his betrothed with a gift as an assurance and reminder of His guaranteed return for her:

- "But wait for the gift my Father promised" (Acts 1:4b).
- "And you will receive the gift of the Holy Spirit" (Acts 2:28).
- "Having believed, you were marked in him with a seal, the promised Holy Spirit, who is a deposit guaranteeing our inheritance until the redemption of those who are God's possession—to the praise of his glory" (Ephesians 1:13c-14).

At this point, only the bridegroom has the authority to annul the contract:

- "God has said, 'Never will I leave you; never will I forsake you'" (Hebrews 13:5b).

The bridegroom returns to His Father's house to prepare a place for His bride:

- "In my Father's house are many rooms; if it were not so, I would have told you. I am going there to prepare a place for you. And if I go and prepare a place for you, I will come back and take you to be with me that you also may be where I am" (John 14:2–3).

Only the Father could make the pronouncement of when the work was complete and give permission for the Bridegroom to go and get His bride:

- "No one knows about that day or hour, not even the angels in heaven, nor the Son, but only the Father" (Matthew 24:36).

This is where we are on the kingdom calendar—betrothed to Christ but waiting for the consummation, our unity with Christ, to be accomplished. Jesus paid it all to call you His bride. He is currently at work, preparing a place for you. And we have our own work to do; this is serious business, and that's what our homework will be about this week. He is coming; He's coming for you/me. He expects us to be waiting, watching, prepared. Our attitude and diligence should not be any less enthusiastic, fervent, or passionate than his!

I left off one very important element of the Jewish wedding ceremony. Do you remember that when the father of the groom was not able to go in search of a bride for his son he would send a trusted representative who then served as a marriage broker or matchmaker? Well, that's us!

"The Spirit and the Bride say, 'Come!'" Revelation 22:17.

THE HOLY WEDDING

WEEK 3
"GOD'S NEW THING"

DAY 1

As seen in the Old Testament, amid discipline and judgments for the people's sinful failures, were promises of grace for a future hope.

- Satan was able to bring down all of mankind and hold them captive, but one was foretold who would destroy Satan (Genesis 3:15).
- The substitutionary sacrifice God provided for Abraham's son foretold of the one to come as a sacrifice for many—God's own Son, the Lamb of God (Genesis 22:13).
- Moses served faithfully as a prophet and mediator but was unable to keep the people from disobedience. One would come like him from among His own brothers to intervene and work salvation (Deuteronomy 18:15, Isaiah 59:16).
- The covenant written on tablets of stone was humanly impossible to obey, but a new covenant was foretold that would be written on the minds and hearts of people who would be empowered by God's Spirit to obey (Jeremiah 31:33b, Ezekiel 36:26–27).
- Mankind's sinful nature brought death into the world. One would come who could redeem them from sin and give everlasting life (Isaiah 59:20; Jeremiah 33:8).
- Israel was God's chosen people, set apart for His glory, but a Servant was coming who would offer the light of salvation to all the world (Isaiah 49:6).

The prophet Malachi left God's people with these hopeful words: "See, I will send my messenger, who will prepare the way before me. Then suddenly the Lord you are seeking will come to his temple; the messenger of the covenant, whom you desire, will come," says the Lord Almighty (Malachi 3:1).

Then four hundred years...(the sound of crickets).

The people of Israel are awaiting the Messiah, the Savior, and before Him would be one announcing His coming, the friend of the Bridegroom. Scripture reveals a good deal about the messenger.

Turn to Isaiah chapter 40. What do you remember from our previous lesson about the significance of this chapter?

_____.

What prophesy does verse 40:3 give?

_____.

Read Matthew 3:1–3, Mark 1:2–4, and John 1:22–23. Who is the messenger?

_____.

Luke 3:15 reveals the people were anticipating the coming of Messiah. How were they "waiting"?

_____.

What were they wondering?

_____.

How does John answer this question (John 1:20)?

_____.

Malachi 4:5 gives a name to the messenger. Who was it they should expect?

_____.

How is Elijah described in 2 Kings 1:8?

_____.

Now, write Matthew's description of John the Baptist in 3:4:

_____.

Read John 1:31. Why does the text say John was baptizing?

_____.

What kind of baptism did John perform? (See Luke 3:3.)

_____.

How would you understand this baptism might assist in the revealing of Christ?

_____.

Remember Elijah's display before the Israelites entreating them to turn from their idol worship and return to the one true God. Like Elijah, John's message is also a call to repentance that would "prepare the way for the Lord."

Then, as now, Christ will not be revealed to an unrepentant heart. Isaiah states that sin keeps God at a distance; it causes Him to hide His face and not listen (Isaiah 59:1–2). But David tells us that God does not despise a broken and contrite heart (Psalm 51:17). A repentant heart is imperative. We must agree with God about our sinful state; otherwise, there is no need for a savior.

Read Matthew 3:11 and John 1:29. How does John the Baptist portray Jesus?

_____.

What distinction does he make regarding John's baptism and Jesus's (Matthew 3:11, Luke 3:16)?

_____.

Back to Malachi 3:1. Who does the verse say will suddenly come?

_____.

There would be no more prophets; they should expect the Lord Himself! Hebrews 1:1 says, "In the past God spoke to our forefathers through the prophets at many times and in various ways, but in these last days he has spoken to us by his Son, whom he appointed heir of all things, and through whom he made the universe."

The Lord is described in the last part of the verse (Malachi 3:1) as "The messenger of the _____." God promised to and did send Jesus to mediate a new covenant of peace between God and man by grace.

The closing words of the Old Testament make mention of both Elijah and Moses: "Remember the law of my servant Moses, the decrees and laws I gave him at Horeb for all Israel" (Malachi 4:4). This seems a bit random, a little out of place here. But as final words before a long silence, this would absolutely be what he would want to leave them with to contemplate and remember. Sinai (which is the same as Horeb) was where God permanently joined Himself to Israel by covenant, with Moses as the mediator of that covenant. Moses had prophesied that the coming Messiah would be like him (Deuteronomy 18:15 and 18).

State the similarities between Moses and Jesus based on the following scriptures:

Exodus 2 and Matthew 2:13–23: _____.

Hebrews 11:24–25 and Philippians 2:5–8:

_____

_____.

Exodus 19:7, 20:19, 35:1; Deuteronomy 29:1; and Hebrews 8:6, 9:15, 12:24:

_____.

Exodus 32:11–13 and 30–32, 33:15; Deuteronomy 9:18; Hebrews 7:25b:

_____

_____.

Exodus 33:11; John 1:1–2 and 14, 8:16 and 29, 10:30, 17:22–23:

_____.

Deuteronomy 18:15b and Matthew 17:5c: _____.

Those alert and watching for Messiah would see it in Jesus by His likeness to Moses.

Elijah and Moses are significant figures not just in the Old Testament but in the New Testament as well. Both of them met God on Mount Sinai (Exodus 3:1, 1 Kings 19:8–18). They both will meet with Jesus on the Mount of Transfiguration (Matthew 17:1–5), and many understand them to be the two witnesses mentioned in Revelation (11:3–12).

The picture God began—the image of His creative purpose to take to Himself a people—that appeared as if it should be discarded has come out from under the drop cloth. What was only a hint of reality now begins to take shape under the Artist's hand; a tangible picture is emerging. The failed attempts of the past for a covenantal love relationship between God and mankind were not mistakes to be wiped away or painted over; they provide depth and dimension as they stand in contrast to the grace that's developing on the canvas of God's story.

Write Galatians 4:4–5:

_____

_____

_____.

"But when the set time had fully come." What do these words indicate to you?

_____.

Jesus was no plan B; the only option left after this colossal flop. We have surely seen from all we've looked at this week how precisely He fits into the picture. Christ was in the original blueprint. Galatians 4:4 states three significant things about Jesus. Fill in the blanks:

Jesus is God's _____. He is born of a _____. He is born under _____.

Each of these characteristics was necessary for the Messiah. Why is that?

_____

_____

_____.

The covenant between God and man was broken. God Himself would provide the one to redeem it and mediate a new one. He would have to be under the constraints of the law in order to fulfill their terms. He would have to be divine to be able to satisfy the demands requiring perfection, and He must be flesh and blood to comply with man's part in the covenant. All three of these positions had to come into play to bring about mankind's redemption from the bondage of the law into the freedom of sons. The second person of the triune God humbled Himself and became flesh and blood. He relinquished the glory and perfection of heaven to live in a fallen, evil world under the constraints of the law. Jesus, in His perfect righteousness, fulfilled the law (Matthew 5:17) and brought a righteousness apart from the law (Romans 3:21) to all those who trust in and receive His redeeming work by faith. God would assume the role of both relationship partners. Instead of a relationship between God and man, it would be a relationship between God and the God-man, Jesus Christ. "Only a covenant based on God's free gift of grace to us in Christ could actually achieve God's purpose to make us a holy people." ("Is Jesus in the Old Testament," Iaian Duguid)

DAY 2

The intent of the law was never to be the means by which people could gain God's favor through their own righteous acts. Read Romans 4:13 and 7:7b. What do these verses state the law was intended to do: _____.

The law revealed our need for a Savior. The end of the law, its goal and fulfillment, was Christ. "Christ is the end of the law so that there may be righteousness for everyone who believes" (Romans 10:4). Righteousness comes by being united by faith in Christ and trusting in His work on our behalf, not anything we do on our own.

Let's look at some aspects of the new covenant expressed by Old Testament prophets:

- When Isaiah spoke about this new covenant and a Servant who would come to gather Israel back to Himself, he also stated that restoring Israel alone would be "too small a thing." The Servant would also be a light for the Gentiles and an offer of salvation to the whole earth (Isaiah 49:5–6).
- The new covenant Jeremiah prophesied about was at hand. The first covenant was written on stone; it was external, a code of conduct. The new covenant is written on hearts and minds; it's internal.
- The prophet Ezekiel told the means by which God would accomplish the ability for an intimate relationship with His people. "I will sprinkle clean water on you, and you will be clean; I will cleanse you from all your impurities and from all your idols. I will give you a new heart and put a new spirit in you; I will remove from you your heart of stone and give you a heart of flesh. And I will put my Spirit in you and move you to follow my decrees and be careful to keep my laws" (Ezekiel 36:25–27).

The new covenant provided that salvation would be offered to all people, not just the Jews. It would be internal, an inward transformation which God Himself, by His Spirit, will work in His people. It offers the cleansing from sin not just covering over it for a time. Finally, it at last provides for the true intimacy God has always desired with His people.

The gospels declare the good news of the great light that has now dawned on those living in darkness. Christ, the Bridegroom, has come to betroth to Himself a bride. The friend of the Bridegroom (John) is going before Jesus, announcing His coming and preparing the way for Him. So Jesus, the "expected" one, officially launches His ministry. After His baptism and wilderness testing, He begins His public ministry and gathers twelve disciples. Not by coincidence, His first miracle takes place at a wedding, and this story is wrought with symbolism.

John 20:30–31 tells us that Jesus performed a number of miracles that were not recorded, but those that are have intent. What is their purpose?

_____

_____.

The reason miracles are recorded is to change us. What difference is there between us and the demons if all we do is believe they occurred? They are intended to increase our faith and incite change in our mind and actions. Read the account in John 2:1–11.

What do you think of Jesus's choice of word to His mother in the first part of verse 4? What was He saying?

_____

_____.

Jesus was not being disrespectful in calling His mother *woman*; it was a common term, sort of like *ma'am*. But He was indicating that the relationship had a different dimension now; He was not functioning as her son but God's—her Messiah. He was also expressing His purpose, which was to do His Father's will. He was no longer under her authority, but God's and His actions would be in accordance with God's mission.

Running out of wine at a wedding would be tremendously humiliating for the bridegroom. Is this what motivated Mary to mention it to Jesus? We don't know, but I do think the text indicates that she believed He would help and she acted in faith by telling the servants to follow His orders. Based on Jesus's response to her initial statement, why do you suppose He took action?

_____

_____

_____.

Jesus cannot be coerced; He does only His Father's will (John 5:19). But is it possible that Jesus's actions were a response to her faith? Scriptures says that without faith it is impossible to please God, which leads to the conclusion that God is pleased when faith is shown.

In addition, this is a wedding; the institution God has created to portray His relationship with His people. Because the wine has run out, social disgrace will fall on this couple that will be remembered for years to come. Since wine symbolizes joy, the deficiency could indicate that neither the bride and groom nor the guests were happy. The shortage might also imply the couple could not sustain the relationship. Very possibly, Jesus was thinking about His bride, the church. A shameful, joyless, weak marriage would not be a good representation of the honorable, joyful, strong, and abundant relationship He would have with His bride. Could this be why He intervened?

The end of the account, verse 11, states that, through this first miracle, Jesus was revealing His glory. The Greek word translated as glory is *doxa*, and it means "to recognize a person or thing for what it is; an opinion, estimate, whether good or bad concerning someone." So through this miracle, Jesus was revealing Himself in order that those around Him could recognize His deity, form a correct opinion of who He really is.

With that purpose in mind, what glory do you see revealed in Jesus by this miracle?

_____

_____.

This being the initial miracle in the inauguration of His ministry, we have to know it's meant to reveal something extraordinary. I am incapable of reaching the depths to be plumbed here, but I did arrive at two basic observations.

First, *Jesus is revealing Himself as our joy.* Weddings are joyful events for all involved, but that was about to be spoiled. Jesus supernaturally supplied the symbol of joy—the wine. Wine was considered a blessing from the Lord (Deuteronomy 7:13), and lack of it was regarded as a curse (Deuteronomy 28:39). Jesus is the joy giver. Jesus concerned Himself with everyone's enjoyment; He wanted them joyful.

Notice the jars Jesus filled with wine were those used for the Jewish ritual of purification. The Jewish religion had no joy, no gladness—no wine. All it could provide was water to wash the body. Jesus not only provided what was lacking; He delighted to provide more than enough. The verses tell us that, minimally speaking, the jars would have held 120 gallons of wine. That estimates to approximately two thousand four-ounce glasses!

This overabundance calls to attention His claim in John 10:10b. What does He say?

_____.

Wine can make the heart glad (Psalm 104:15 and Zechariah 10:7), but Jesus makes it supremely glad. He is the greater joy. Other sources of joy will always run out and prove to be deficient, but Jesus is the source; His supply is inexhaustible.

We are designed for joy. We need it, but it has to come from Christ. No other pleasure can hold up to the demand. Finding joy through God's gifts and creation is good and right, but oftentimes, what was intended to point us back to Him, the source of all beauty and joy, becomes a means unto itself. We pursue joy through relationships, food, wine, art, scenery, etc. If we make them the source of our joy, we will destroy them by demanding what they were never designed to give. Jesus's miracle demonstrates this clearly. His first miracle was to provide what the bridegroom at the wedding could not provide. The bridegroom was responsible for the wine, and he had let it run out. Even the best bridegrooms will fail, but Jesus is the never-failing, abundantly supplying bridegroom.

Of course, we realize that joy and happiness are not equals. The currently popular prosperity gospel offers a cheap substitute for the deep abiding joy that is ours in Christ. The happiness that they insist should be the norm for Christians is substandard to Christ's real offer. Being happy is good; Proverbs 15:13 says a happy heart makes the face cheerful. This is clearly news to some Christians! But happiness cannot be sustained through all circumstances; joy is an enduring treasure, a gift from God.

Jesus wants you to be joyful. He has provided by His indwelling Spirit for that to be possible.

What is your source of joy (and don't just give the appropriate "church" answer; when in doubt say, "Jesus"). Be honest. Where do you find joy?

_____

_____

_____

_____.

If it were taken away, would it affect your joyfulness?

_____.

Many times, we don't realize we've allowed the beauty around us and the magnificent things God has provided to become our source of joy. We lose sight of the fact that the "things" are simply extension of His goodness, His love, and His mercy. Things will fail. Relationships will disappoint. Too much food and wine will have a negative effect. The pursuit of leisure, travel, or thrills cannot sustain. But Jesus says our joy can be complete in Him (John 15:11). God made us with longings—a desire and yearning for more. With Christ there is always more; we will never exhaust the wonders of His person.

DAY 3

The second observation is *Jesus is revealing Himself as our salvation.*

Jesus gives a strange answer to Mary's request in John 2:4b. What did He say?

_____.

Read John 7:30, 8:20, 12:23 and 27, 13:1, and 17:1. What do these verses tell you about His "hour"? What hour is He talking about?

_____.

Don't you find Jesus's reply to Mary odd?
Mary said, "Jesus, these poor people have run out of wine. Oh my, how humiliating!"
Jesus replied, "Ma'am, why are you bringing this up now? It isn't my time to die."
The "hour" Jesus speaks of refers to His death and resurrection. Jesus's purpose, His mission from God, was to give His life for what will be His bride. Although the climax of His ministry is not at hand, it's almost like He says, "But since it's come up, I'll illustrate for you what it will mean."

What does Jesus instruct the servants to do in verse 7?

_____.

What were the jars traditionally used for?

_____.

Jesus specifically calls for the servants to use the jars meant for ceremonial washing. Surely there were water jars around that could have been used, but that's not what He chose. Maybe you've been taught that this verse shows God will utilize whatever or whoever is available. Some teach that Jesus looked around, spotted what was available and that's what He employed. While the substance of that is true, God can and does use "cracked pots" and anything else, it's absolutely not what happened in this instance. Jesus was very intentional.

In addition to the representation of joy, wine also symbolizes the blood of Christ (Matthew 26:27–28; John 6:53 and 55). Jesus fills the jars intended for purification, required by the law, with wine. He was revealing that by His blood, He would provide purification for sin that the law could not provide. Jesus' "hour" will make the pots irrelevant. His shed blood would be the final and ultimate purification for sins.

There is no longer the need for ceremonial washing that must be done time and time again; but we are however, required to wash. Revelation 22:14 tells us that to have eternal life we must wash our robes.

How does Revelation 7:14 say we can wash our robes and make them white?

_____.

Jesus, the Lamb of God, is the fullness of God's grace through whom we receive one blessing after another (John 1:16). The writer of Hebrews tells us that Christ's ministry of grace is superior to the law (Hebrews 8:6).
- When the law was given at Sinai, three thousand lost their lives (Exodus 32:28). When the message of salvation by grace was given at Pentecost, three thousand received eternal life (Acts 2:41).
- The law reveals we are sinners (Romans 7:7b). Grace covers them (Romans 3:24).
- The law could not make any one perfect (Hebrews 7:18, 10:1). Christ's sacrifice of grace makes perfect forever those who come to Him (Hebrews 19:14).

The law came first, but like the wine Jesus made at the wedding, the best was saved for last. The new covenant initiated by Jesus's completed work on the cross is more excellent in every way to the old—much more. Paul enthusiastically proclaims four times in Romans chapter 5 "how much more" is now attainable through Christ. How much more? Oh, so much more; in every way! John 1:17 says, "For the law came through Moses; grace and truth came through Jesus Christ."

During this particular wedding, surely Jesus was thinking about His own bride and the covenant He would make with her shortly. Read Luke 22:20. What were Jesus and the disciples doing (verse 13)?

_____.

How does He refer to "the cup"?

_____.

Jesus's disciples would have immediately recognized the marriage proposal imagery in sharing the cup together.

There are four cups of blessing in a traditional Passover meal. Each cup represents the "I wills" of God in Exodus 6. Many believe that this particular cup Jesus referred to in Luke 22:20 is the third cup that corresponds with the third "I will" statement.

What does it say (Exodus 6:6, middle of the verse)?

_____.

What was Jesus moving toward; where would He be in a few short hours?

_____.

Drinking the cup sealed the promise. He made a vow, and there would be no turning back. With outstretched arms nailed to a cross, He fulfilled His vows to redeem an ungrateful and uncaring bride. The mighty acts of judgments fell on Him as the bearer of mankind's sin. He absorbed God's fierce wrath until every inch of Him was marred beyond recognition. Jesus drank a cup of wrath so that we may drink from a cup of joy. This cup was extravagantly expensive; it should be cherished, savored, and enjoyed. Jesus is God's best wine; the joy and salvation found in Him alone is the "more" we crave.

Do you have "empty" areas in your life you need Jesus to fill? If so what are they?

_____
_____
_____.

Are there areas, especially spiritually speaking, in which you are just going through the motions but with no joy?

_____
_____
_____.

Ask the Lord to fill you with the joy and satisfaction that can only be found in Him, and expect Him to accomplish it; let it build your faith. At the wedding that day, each person attending was able to have more wine, but some, with eyes to see and ears to hear, were able to have more faith (John 2:9, 11).

Jesus's earthly ministry would begin and end with wine. No wonder the disciples marveled at this. Of course, they were unable to fully grasp the force behind the events, but they had intimate knowledge of the Scriptures and recognized the time of Messiah as an age where wine would flow abundantly (Joel 3:18 and Amos 9:13).

More specifically, how does the prophet Isaiah describe the wine that will be served at the great banquet the Lord will host (Isaiah 25:6)?

_____.

The disciples would not have missed the correlation between Isaiah's prophesy and Jesus's fine wine.

Jesus often used the context of His surroundings to reveal something unique or unknown about Himself.

- While in a great storm on the water, He used the setting to reveal His power over nature.
- While teaching from a boat in the water, He noticed the net and used the setting to reveal His power over the fish.
- Twice while teaching a large crowd on a hillside, He used the setting to reveal His power to supernaturally provide food.
- At a funeral, He used the setting to reveal His power over death.
- And many times He chose to heal in the setting of the Sabbath to reveal that His new covenant was one of mercy (hesed) rather than sacrifice.

Just like those, Jesus will use the backdrop of this wedding to reveal Himself as the Bridegroom. The provision of wine was the bridegroom's duty. By taking responsibility, Jesus was making a statement.

Matthew 9:14–15. How does Jesus describe Himself?

_____.

Read John 3:27–30. What does John the Baptist call Jesus?

_____.

How does John relate to the Bridegroom?

_____.

Who is the bride in verse 29?

_____.

DAY 4

Jesus's teachings were challenging, especially to those who were prospering under the regulations of the law. Jesus had an especially direct confrontation with the religious elite of the day that will mean more to you after last week's lesson. Read Matthew 21:33–46.

Jesus is clearly alluding to the passage in Isaiah 5 that describes Israel as the vineyard and God as the owner. If you remember, everything had been provided by God to insure good fruit but it produced only bad. The chief priests and elders would have recognized that immediately.

Who are the "tenants" in this parable, the ones given responsibility for the vineyard's care?

_____.

Who did the "servants" represent?

_____.

Who was the last one sent?

_____.

Based on the response of these Jewish leaders in verse 41, do you think they understood who was represented? Did they see themselves? Why or why not?

_____

_____.

These men condemned themselves with their response. Indeed, other tenants will be brought in who will produce fruit. The gospel was preached first to the Jews, but at their rejection, it came to the Gentiles. God is seeking fruit.

What does John 15:8 say happens when we bear much fruit?

_____.

The natural vine produced no good fruit so the Gentiles, the church, were grafted in to bring forth fruit (Romans 11). Once again, Jesus speaks to these same people; this time using a wedding parable. The previous parable applied Old Testament prophecy while this next parable is prophetic in nature, describing current events as well as future. Read Matthew 22:1–14.

Who is the wedding banquet for?

_____.

Invitations had gone out. What an enormous honor to be included in this wedding celebration; what was the response of those invited?

_____.

At what point were they entreated again to come (verse 4)?

_____.

How did they respond to this last invitation?

_____.

Remembering Jesus's audience, what was He trying to make them understand?

_____

_____.

The Jewish people were the first to be invited to the wedding of the Son of God, the King. Jesus Himself brought the gospel to them, but they refused it. When everything had been made ready at the sacrifice of Jesus's death, God in His gracious patience continued to call them through His servants the Apostles. They were met with rejection, abuse, and even death. The enraged king's destructive actions foretold the devastation of Jerusalem in AD 70 as God's judgment on the nation of Israel for rejecting His Son. This parable, like the previous one, illustrates how Gentiles became a part of the "guest list" that would usher in the church age. Early on in Israel's history the Lord foretold His intent.

Read Deuteronomy 32:21. What two emotions does God express here and why?

_____.

Because of this, what does He purpose to do?

_____.

Paul's letter to the Romans expresses this very thing. What does he say (Romans 11:11)?

_____.

Do these verses surprise you? Does it make the Lord seem petty and vindictive? From a human perspective, it can be perceived that way, but we must always remember that God simply cannot act apart from love. God has not "divorced" Israel. He hates divorce (Malachi 2:16). He's just giving her some much needed time to think.

Read Isaiah 65:1. If the people referred to in this verse (the Gentiles) were neither seeking God nor asking for Him, how was it they would come to know Him?

_____.

Motivated purely by grace, God offered the church communion with Himself. The effort was all His, as the scripture indicates. They weren't even looking for Him. Who can conceive the grace and mercy of God? A people, underserving and ill-prepared for participation in the things of God, were invited into an intimate relationship with a Holy God. To the Jews, who credited their lineage and submission to the law for being the chosen ones of God, this was inconceivable. They were negligent in recognizing that there is no one righteous (Ecclesiastes 7:20), and their blood sacrifices had no ability to take away their sins (Hebrews 10:4), which is why they had to continue year after year.

Since "those invited" were not interested, who does verse 9–10 say the call was extended to?

_____.

The church is by no means an elite group; it appears the only qualification is to have a heartbeat! The parable, however, discloses an essential requirement. What did the King find that made Him angry (verse 11–12)?

_____.

These invitees had been pulled off the streets, so why would this man be so harshly condemned for having the wrong clothes?

_____.

Since the wedding banquet attendees were bid to come just as they are, the king would have provided appropriate wedding clothes. The attention now turns from the Jewish nation's rejection of Jesus to the criteria for those coming to Christ.

The man in his "street clothes" at the wedding banquet had clearly rejected the king's offered garments, deciding his own would be sufficient. His decision was beyond presumptuous; this was a royal wedding, the son of a king! Just a few short years ago, we witnessed all the grandeur a royal wedding brings when Prince William married Kate Middleton; there was not one invited guest there in Dockers.

The heart of the new covenant is the gift of imputed righteousness, the great exchange. Isaiah 61:10 prophesied this provision of clothing. What garments does this verse say are provided?

_____.

What are these adornments likened to?

_____.

The gospel invitation is open to everyone to come just as they are, but it must be with the realization that you are unacceptably dressed. In fact, the awareness should cause an utter sense of mourning. The deep desire to accept this gracious invitation, coupled with the awareness that your unacceptable appearance, is devastating. Entrance into the celebration will involve a garment only the king can provide.

What does Romans 13:14 say this garment must be?

_____.

Paul explains this issue well in Romans 9:30–31 and 10:3–4. Read it and describe in your own words who got it right, who got it wrong, and why.

_____
_____
_____
_____
_____.

The Jewish people are not the only ones presuming a righteousness of their own making; many in the church are doing the same thing. And it is the church that Jesus continues speaking to in this parable.

What does the king call the inappropriately dressed man (Matthew 22:12)?

_____.

It's not clear, but do you get the impression any of the other guests have noticed a problem with his attire?

_____.

After being questioned about his lack of acceptable attire, how does the man defend himself?

_____.

What are Jesus's words of summation in verse 14?

_____.

Many are invited to the wedding feast. They may be friendly toward the gospel and by all outward appearances look as if they belong, possibly even believing they do. But without the clothes of righteousness imputed through faith in Jesus Christ, they will be thrown out into darkness. Jesus speaks of a similar group of people in Matthew 7:21–23.

Just prior to that, in Matthew 7:13–14, Jesus specifies the way into God's kingdom. What does it say?

_____.

These verses refer to two gates, each leading to very different places. It demands a decision; a choice must be made. The gate and road accessing eternal life is narrow, which means constricted, hemmed in; it's a very tight squeeze. Those choosing this road can bring nothing with them. No achievements, no shame, no self-righteousness—nothing.

According to Jesus, how many choose this road?

_____.

Based on Matthew 7:14 and 22:14, why do you suppose only a few receive eternal life when the invitation is so generous and open to all?

_____.

Receiving an invitation (the gospel) to the wedding banquet of the king's son (life with Christ) demands an RSVP; it requires an intentional decision. An acceptance will mean adherence to the specifications—appropriate attire required. You can absolutely come as you are. You just can't stay that way.

What is more, the church is not only an invited guest, an honor in itself, but the much-cherished bride. Her groom is a valiant King who is virtuous and just and splendid in His beauty with a fiery passion for His bride. The ferocity of His immeasurable love will compel Him to surrender His life on her behalf. The picture of marriage, that God the Father designed and established back in Eden, is accomplished in its display of the new covenant between Christ and the church.

Jesus has come to fulfill the old covenant and institute a new one. The old covenant required a blood sacrifice to atone for the sins of the people: "Without the shedding of blood there is no forgiveness" (Hebrews 9:22).

DAY 5

Another foreshadowing of a coming Savior in the Old Testament were the feasts of the Lord. We'll only have time to hit the highlights of the first four, but perhaps it will spark an interest; they are a tremendously interesting topic of study. The Lord had set up seven major feasts the Israelites were to celebrate (Leviticus 23:2). Four of them were in the spring and three in the fall. They were sacred ceremonies rich in prophetic meaning that God commanded them to observe. *Feast* means appointed time, appointed place, appointed meeting. God carefully planned and orchestrated each of them to reveal an extraordinary story.

The first of these feasts was Passover. It was meant to call to remembrance how God caused the angel of *death to pass over* the firstborn of Israel and *delivered them out of slavery*. It was a *yearly* commemoration in which they would choose *a perfect, unblemished lamb with no broken bones* to be sacrificed as atonement for their sins.

Jesus was crucified on the day of preparation for the Passover (John 19:31) when the lambs would be slaughtered.

What is Jesus called in 1 Corinthians 5:7b?

_____.

How does 1 Peter 1:19 describe Him?

_____.

What important fact is stated in John 19:33b?

_____.

2 Tim 1:10 confirms that Jesus Christ, our Savior, destroyed

_____.

Galatians 4:7 say we were taken from _____ to _____.

According to Hebrews 10:10, how many times would Jesus need to be sacrificed?

_____.

Who could His blood sacrifice be applied to?

_____.

The second feast was Unleavened Bread, celebrated the day following Passover. It was to be a sacred assembly when they did no regular work. The feast began with the offering of the first sheaths of grain to celebrate God's *provision of bread*. During the seven-day celebration, the bread, called the *bread of affliction*, could *contain no leaven* (symbolic of sin and corruption) in remembrance of Israel's hasty exodus from Egypt when their bread had no time to rise.

The day after Passover, the Feast of Unleavened Bread, Jesus lay in the grave. How does Jesus describe Himself in John 6:35?

_____.

Hebrews 4:15 says that although Jesus was tempted in every way we are, He had no

_____.

Isaiah 53:4–5 tells us that Jesus was smitten by God and _____. He was pierced and crushed for our sin. By His _____ we are healed.

The third feast was to take place *the day after the Sabbath*, the Feast of First Fruits. This was the *beginning of the harvest*, and it was to acknowledge and celebrate God's provision from the earth. The people were to bring the first of their harvest before the priest who would wave it before the Lord in the temple. Only after this was done could the crops be harvested and used. When does Matthew 28:1 tell us Jesus was resurrected?

_____.

What is Jesus called in 1 Corinthians 15:20?

_____.

Firstfruit of what?

_____.

What sort of harvest does Romans 8:29 indicate He is the first of?

_____.

The fourth and final spring feast was Pentecost or Feast of Weeks. It took place seven weeks or fifty days after the Feast of Firstfruits. Pentecost means fifty, which is how it acquired its name. The feast celebrated the wheat harvest as well as the anniversary of the giving of the Torah on Mount Sinai. The people were to bring an offering of grain along with two loaves of bread baked with yeast.

Read Acts 2:1–11. What day does this narrative take place?

_____.

While the disciples were all together, what did they receive (verse 4)?

_____.

Who was around to witness the commotion (verse 5)?

_____.

God's presence on Mount Sinai, at the giving of the law, was accompanied by fire, smoke, and the sound of thunder (Hebrew for thunder means "voices"). What similar expressions of God's presence at the giving of the Holy Spirit did the disciples and others experience (verse 2–4 and 11)?

_____.

After Peter's explanation (verse 14–36), what was the response from the people according to verse 37?

_____.

Based on your observations above, what do you believe was God's purpose in requiring bread with yeast as an offering?

_____.

The Torah, or law, was given on Pentecost. Torah means teaching. It was much more than rules to follow; it was meant to teach them how to live. What does John 14:26 say the Holy Spirit will do?

_____.

The Feasts of the Lord were established by God in the earliest stages of Israel's history, some 1,400 plus years before Christ. Of the seven, we've observed the four feasts celebrated in the spring; each of which found their complete fulfillment in Christ. What does Colossians 2:17 tells us these are?

_____.

The crucifixion of Jesus took place at the exact time of the afternoon sacrifice. A lamb was chosen to be sacrificed "for the nation." It was staked out in the temple courtyard at 9:00 a.m. on Passover and publicly slaughtered at 3:00 p.m. when the high priest cut the throat of the lamb, saying these words, "It is finished." Jesus, the Lamb of God, was nailed to the cross at 9:00 a.m. (Mark 15:25) and died at 3:00 p.m. (Mark 15:34). As the shofar blew, filling Jerusalem with the sound announcing that sacrifices had been made, Jesus shouted, "It is finished!"

The sacred assembly of the Feast of Unleavened Bread found the Bread of Life (John 6:35), who knew no sin, hidden away in a tomb after eating the bread of affliction. But because He had no "yeast," His body would not see decay. As the next day dawned to celebrate the Feast of Firstfruits, the one and only Son of God rose from the grave, the firstfruit of a coming harvest. He is the first among many brothers (Romans 8:29) to be taken from death to life.

Fifty days later, the Holy Spirit falls on the disciples with a violent wind and tongues of fire, evoking John the Baptist's characterization of the baptism Jesus would do—with the Holy Spirit and with fire! What a harvest celebration this Pentecost would turn out to be as God had prepared Jerusalem to be filled with people from "every nation under heaven" to witness this wonder. By enabling the disciples to miraculously speak in foreign languages, every person would hear the gospel in their own tongue, equipping them to return to their own land to spread the good news. Just as the commanded offering of bread would contain yeast, so would this harvest of people. But the fire of the Holy Spirit indwelling those receiving the gospel will set them free from the bondage of sin (2 Corinthians 3:17) and display the glory of God by working in them to will and to act according to God's good purpose (Philippians 2:13).

As we've stated from day 1, God's desire and design was always to live among His people in an intimate relationship. In summary; although the whole earth is filled with His glory, God manifested His presence among His beloved in a special visual way in order for them to know He was living among them. Let's look at its progression:

As God led the Israelites out of Egypt, how did He reveal His presence (Exodus 13:21)?

_____.

When making the covenant (marrying) with Israel, describe the manifestation of His presence (Exodus 19:16 and 18).

_____.

How did God display His presence at the completion of the tabernacle, where God would dwell among His people (Exodus 40:34 and 38)?

_____.

After the completion of Solomon's magnificent temple, built for the Lord's dwelling, what happened according to 2 Chronicles 7:1?

_____.

How does Ezekiel describe God's manifest presence that eventually departs from Israel (Ezekiel 1:4 and 13)?

_____.

Finally, what are the indications that God's presence, His glory, has returned based on Acts 2:2–4?

_____.

This day of Pentecost marks the beginning of the church. The glory of God—His manifest presence that had first filled the tabernacle in the wilderness, then Solomon's temple, and departed from His people some six hundred years earlier—now returns. The glory of God currently resides in the bodies of believers. The presence of God would not live in the holy of holies but would dwell directly within His people. What a truly awesome achievement!

When God's glory filled Solomon's temple, what was Solomon's response (1 Kings 8:27)?

_____

_____.

Solomon marveled at the fact that God, in all His splendor and majesty, great and mighty, Most High, would condescend to dwell in a mere temple. How could He possibly squeeze all His Godness into such a small place, magnificent as it was? So I want to ask you, how much more should we be in awe that all His glory could and would indwell us?

The temple curtain separating the presence of God and His people was suddenly and supernaturally ripped in two at the death of Jesus. His glorious presence once available to the people only through the high priest once a year now fills those who receive His sanctifying work.

The actuality of the Lord's desire to dwell with His people, to be their God and take them to Himself, is at hand.

Read Ephesians 5:25–32. God instituted marriage in order to use something we know, that we can see and understand, to reveal something conceptual or intangible.

To what does Paul compare Christ's love for the church (verse 25)?

_____.

In the comparison, what role does He (Christ) assume?

_____.

What pronoun does he use to describe the church (verse 27)?

_____.

For what purpose did Christ sanctify the church?

_____.

How do verses 25b–26a say He made her holy?

_____.

How is she cleansed (verse 26)?

_____.

I *love* the visual these words convey! This is the ideal Cinderella story. We've spent three weeks examining this bride, and she is stained, wrinkled, and blemished. God's own descriptions of her in the Old Testament were very frank, especially if you have the ESV! And listen, we are just like her; we are no different. A profound mystery, indeed! The God who is holy, holy, holy cannot overlook the fact that she is far from clean, holy, or blameless. How can He become one with her when His own word speaks against being united with a prostitute (1 Corinthians 6:15–16)? He cleans her up Himself.

God the Father set the price for this unworthy, unlovely bride. God the Son paid it with His own precious blood, thus sanctifying her. God the Spirit, the gift to believers, makes her one with Christ. This promises to be a beautiful wedding. Listen to a description based on Psalm 45:

The Bridegroom is the most handsome of men; His lips anointed with grace. He is mighty, clothed in splendor and majesty. He rides in victory on behalf of truth, humility, and righteousness; His right hand displaying awesome deeds. He is righteous and just; therefore, God has exalted Him and anointed Him with the oil of joy.

This magnificent Groom, at great cost to Himself, cleanses His beloved from every stain and blemish. He presents her to Himself, holy and blameless. She leaves the past behind and is now a royal bride, and she is radiant! Gloriously dressed in the finest gold and embroidered garments, she is led to her King. He is enthralled by her beauty. There is great joy and gladness as they enter the palace of the King.

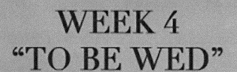

THE HOLY WEDDING

DAY 1

If you are a Christian, you are part of the body of Christ and betrothed to Jesus. We have entered into a relationship with Him and vowed to love Him and serve Him alone. We have promised to be faithful to Him alone. At our baptism, we pledged not to forsake our first love, and we became His bride.

God's picture of His true purpose for marriage is almost complete. The initial image on this grand work of art depicted a sleeping Adam with a God-inflicted wound from which Adam's bride would be created. As it turns out, that image was just a shadow to the true image that has come into view of Christ "sleeping" in a tomb, wounded and afflicted by God for the purpose of bringing forth His bride.

This picture places a much more significant meaning for me to Paul's words in 1 Corinthians 6:19c–20a. Write it here:

_____.

Does this truth mean more to you than it did previous to this study; if so, why?

_____.

Jesus has betrothed to Himself a bride. The marriage proposal has been sealed with the blood of the new covenant. He has gone to prepare a place for her and, at His Father's command, will return to receive His bride and be united with her forever. In the interim, He has left her with something very important; a bridal gift. This gift, akin to our modern-day engagement ring, was to assure His bride of His return.

What is the gift or promise the Lord assured He would give (Luke 24:49, Acts 1:4–5 and 2:38)?

_____.

What are we told in 2 Corinthians 1:22 the purpose of this gift is?

_____.

The Lord has put what equates to be earnest money down on His bride. He's made a deposit, and her status is certain for "the day of redemption" (Ephesians 4:30).

Meanwhile, the bride is to be preparing for His return. We, the church, are brides-to-be, preparing for a wedding. Our preparations are not just for a wedding ceremony; we are also preparing to be a wife . . . of a king. Let that seep in for a minute. This is more than a lovely thought or romantic illustration; it's a stark reality. What an amazing honor . . . and a terrifying truth! Girl, we've got some preparing to do! Let's start with Jesus's parable on this very subject.

In Matthew 25, Jesus is telling a parable (actually, more than one) in response to a question. Look back to Matthew 24:3 and write the question:

_____.

Jesus, our Bridegroom, could literally come at any moment. Do you consider yourself prepared for that?

Weddings are a significant event, especially in today's times. Brides undergo a lot of pressure in preparation. I've never heard of a bride to just throw something on, run a brush through her hair, add a little lipstick, and a breath mint, and consider herself ready to be married. I will say, however, that if television is any indication, the wedding is the only area of a marriage that today's bride concerns herself with. But the "big day" is a big deal. Brides, of even the most modest means, are often incredibly extravagant. No expense is spared for the dress, shoes, jewelry, etc. The hair and makeup professionals cannot show up just on the big day. No . . . there must be practice sessions. And any remaining time will need to be spent on areas to be waxed and plucked, along with the essential mani-pedi.

This (slightly exaggerated) depiction is the accepted and expected way for a modern bride to prepare for her wedding day. There is nothing essentially wrong with this picture, but in contrast, how much time, effort, energy, thought, or interest is going into our preparation to meet Jesus, our beautiful groom. His arrival is imminent, and as we will see in this parable, as His bride, we must be prepared and watchful.

Read Matthew 25:1–13. Who are the players in verse 1?

_____.

How are the virgins distinguished and what gave them this distinction (verse 2–4)?

_____.

The text tells us these virgins were waiting expectantly for their bridegroom, but verse 5 says He was _____.

The parable goes on to say the sleepy virgins are awakened to the shout that the Bridegroom had arrived. What did the ten virgins do next (Matthew 25:7–9)?

_____.

How does the story wrap up? What becomes of the five foolish and five wise virgins (verses 10–11)?

_____

_____.

When the foolish virgins arrived at the banquet, what did the bridegroom tell them (verse 12)?

_____.

Let's break this down. Why do they have lamps, what do lamps do?

_____.

Who is light attributed to in these verses: Matthew 5:14 and 16; Acts 13:47; 2 Corinthians 4:6?

_____.

What does the fact that the five foolish virgins brought oil lamps but neglected the very element necessary for them to work indicate to you?

_____.

The bride is a light bearer, bringing the light of the salvation of God into the world. This light is not her own but light given to her through the Holy Spirit. In the Bible, oil is a widely understood symbol of the Holy Spirit. The oil of anointing and the Spirit of the Lord are directly linked. All ten of the virgins have their "light," and all of them are going out to meet the bridegroom. They all have the same mission, and with the exception of the oil, they all appear alike.

With that in mind, who do you understand the ten virgins to represent?

_____.

The ten virgins represent the visible church, and in the church, there are the wise and the foolish.

The bride is not mentioned here, but don't let that trip you up. The virgins represent the bride, the church, who goes out to meet the bridegroom. And the fact that there are ten is not some sort of sanction for polygamy. This parable is to teach that although many may profess Christ and even believe they belong to Him, only those prepared with the necessary equipment are the true bride.

Only one factor separates these otherwise bridegroom enthusiasts: oil. The parable indicates a single responsibility—to have light. Light would provide for them if they were caught off guard. It was not only possible but very probable that a groom would come in the middle of the night. Brides knew that; therefore, they took lamps. As the excited bride went out to meet her groom, the light would show her the way. It would keep her from stumbling. It would help those around her to see; and it would illuminate the face of her beloved. But to have light, you have to have oil—that's a non-negotiable.

How would you depict the five foolish virgins in the church today? Describe them.

_____

_____.

No matter how great one's enthusiasm is for God, how vast one's knowledge or degree of commitment to Him and His people, without the Holy Spirit providing the right perspective, attitude, intention and empowerment, they are lamps without oil—useless. They do not possess the means in which they can know Christ.

The five foolish virgins represent those in the church whose association with Christ is only professed; they have only an outward form of religion. They are the ones who have decided to do things their own way. Consequently they are foolish. God has clearly defined in His Word the specific requirements for salvation. He has not left it up to chance, and we do not get to decide what works best for us.

Clearly, we can see from this parable that possessing the Holy Spirit is vital. Paul gives the church in Corinth specific instructions regarding this subject. Write 2 Corinthians 13:5 here:

_____

_____

_____.

Jesus taught that it won't be because people don't know Him that will keep them from heaven. Many of them will call Him by name. They will be excluded because *He* never knew *them* (Matthew 7:21); the very same words He uses in this parable. The tragedy and heartbreak is that these people are surprised and upset. Listen, ladies. We have to test ourselves. This is not a time to cross your fingers and hope for the best. We have to know for certain because this test is pass or fail. Jesus taught that no matter how a person might appear, proof of their salvation will be in their fruit: "A good tree cannot bear bad fruit, and a bad tree cannot bear good fruit" (Matthew 7:18). We have to do some self-analysis. Will what you are producing stand up to the penetrating scrutiny of the Bridegroom's blazing eyes of fire (Revelation 1:14)? Does He know you?

Jesus says that only those who do the will of His Father enter into God's kingdom, and His stated will is for people to acknowledge Jesus Christ as Savior (Acts 2:21), repent of their sinfulness, receive the Holy Spirit of God (Acts 2:38), and submit to His transforming work of becoming like Christ (Romans 8:29). There is not another way—no shortcuts or substitutes.

Unfortunately, the gospel presentation of previous generations has given false assurance of salvation. Our churches are full of these tragically deceived individuals who have been taught that if you, at any time in your life, prayed a prayer to receive Christ, you're saved. Regardless of whether or not you gave Jesus one more thought or made even the slightest attempt at serving or obeying Him, as long as you said that prayer, you're good. You've got your ticket.

True salvation is not just mental assent because even the demons believe Jesus to be who He says He is. Understanding and acknowledging Jesus as the one and only Son of God is fundamental, but it's not enough. This is where many fall short of saving faith.

On the following lines, write in your own words what you understand it takes to be saved. Please don't move on without doing this. It's very important to be able to express for yourself what you believe and why. It might also be a really good test; maybe, as it turns out, you don't know. Take the time to wrestle through this and put it on paper. _____

_____

_____

_____.

DAY 2

Look again at the parable. The virgins are all sleeping when the bridegroom comes. This parable, as well as the one before and the one after, all point to Jesus's return as taking a very long time. What is the hazard of doing something, seemingly in vain, for a prolonged time?

_____ .

Jesus warns us over and over again, in regard to His return, to keep watch and be ready because He will be coming on a day we are not expecting Him (Matthew 24:44 and 50, 25:13). Being caught a bit off guard did not affect the wise virgins. They had all they needed in order to meet their groom. They were watching and prepared. The five foolish virgins were neither. Their lack of oil was a blatant omission.

What do you think it says about them that when they awoke to the announcement, they trimmed their lamps?

_____ .

It seems to me that they trimmed their lamps with the expectation that these good, sweet, and compassionate fellow virgins could and would share their oil if necessary. What's the problem with that plan?

_____ .

Do you know or have you witnessed people like that who profess to be a Christian just by virtue of their upbringing, the thought being since their parents/grandparent are saved, they obviously are as well? Or those that reason as good, moral people, God will accept them? What about the people who ride the spiritual coattails of a believer, thinking some will rub off? I guess they think that when the trumpet of the Lord sounds, they can just hold on to their ascending friend.

Jesus is coming for His bride. Write 1 Thessalonians 4:16.

_____
_____
_____ .

And Scripture is clear; we won't be expecting Him. Many will stand before Him with empty lamps and hear those terrifying words, "I don't know you." But we don't have to. We have a choice.

Luke 12:35 gives good instructions; write the verse here:

_____.

Look back at last week's lesson. The second-to-last page regarding the manifestation of God's presence. What was the one common factor in them all?

_____.

Believers receive the Holy Spirit one time at our baptism or identification with Christ. Recalling John's words (Matthew 3:11d), this baptism would also come with fire.

The moment we received Christ, a flame was ignited. This flame, like the lampstand in the tabernacle (Exodus 27:20–21), never goes out. It's fueled by the Holy Spirit. We cannot see God, but what was seen of His presence was fire. Fire is not a benign, passive element; fire is threatening, aggressive, and frightening. It consumes. The Israelites were terrified at the sight. In his book *The God Who Smokes*, Timothy Stoner illustrates wonderfully the fiery nature of God:

> And our Groom is a heroic King, a mighty warrior who is good and just and stunning in his beauty. He is so full of passion and blazing emotion that he burns—and yes, smokes in the ferocity of his infinite, holy love that compelled him to give it all away for his Bride. And he who gave it all for us is worth giving ourselves completely to. He is astonishingly beautiful, utterly majestic and perfect in the symmetries of justice and righteousness, knowledge, and wisdom. He is as hypnotically compelling as a surging forest fire and ten times as dangerous. He is out of control—ours, not his. He is a burning cyclone of passionate love.

The Spirit of the God portrayed as "a burning cyclone of passionate love" who "smokes in the ferocity of his infinite, holy love" is the Spirit indwelling us! I know you know that. What I want to ask is, does it look like it? Are you on fire? Does your passionate love for your Groom look anything like His for you?

Hebrews 12:29 describes our God as _____.

God isn't "nice," and He isn't safe. He's fierce and fearsome but not bullying or bad-tempered. His zeal to make us a holy people is a burning passion, a consuming fire! A. W. Tozer says, "We need to take refuge *from* God, *in* God."

Should we not be just as passionately consumed with Him? By Him? Or are we terrified at the thought of it, not wanting to come across as "too much," a Jesus freak who turns people off. Jesus said we are the light of the world, but regrettably, the light of Christ's bride is so dim. No one's attracted to it; it's insufficient to be of any help.

As Christ's bride, our lives should display a fervency for Christ and what He loves. The flame is initiated by God but requires care from us, not in the sense that it could be lost but in its ability to be consistently ablaze.

Read 1 Thessalonians 5:19. What instructions are we given regarding the Holy Spirit?

_____.

What do you understand that to mean? How would that happen? Does it seem contradictory to the truth that the Holy Spirit is a seal, a guarantee, and cannot be removed?

_____.

Fire is extinguished by dousing it with water, depriving it of oxygen or fuel—in other words, from soaking, stifling, or suppressing it. Spiritually speaking, consider the ways we put out the fire of the Holy Spirit.

_____

_____

_____.

Only through the Spirit's power we will be dressed appropriately and beautifully to meet our Bridegroom. Read Revelation 19:7–8. Note a couple of interesting things. How does verse 7 say the bride has accomplished her readiness?

_____.

Where did she get her wedding clothes (verse 8)?

_____.

The fine linen the bride is dressed in is characterized as what?

_____.

The bride's wedding clothes have been given to her; they will be her righteous acts. We certainly know, at this point in our study, that these are not just external efforts. Having no righteousness of our own, these acts/actions derive from the imputed righteousness of Christ. Scripture tells us we do nothing apart from Christ (John 15:5); nothing, that is, that God would deem of value. Any act of merit or significance we do will be under the power and leading of God's Holy Spirit. These will be our clothes—what we will come forth in, dressed to meet our Groom. Some of us may be humiliatingly overexposed from lack of clothing. I'm really not trying to be funny; the scripture says the bride has made *herself* ready. The righteousness is ascribed, but we are to make ourselves ready by loyalty and faithfulness to Christ through obedience to His Word.

Notice, she didn't choose these clothes; they were chosen for her. Like the parable we studied last week, what the bride wears is not only important, it's a deal breaker. What we might reason to be satisfactory or even better garments is not for our choosing; we are to wear what we're given. The old hymn says it well: "When He shall come with trumpet sound, O may I then in Him be found. Dressed in His righteousness alone, faultless to stand before the throne."

Write Matthew 5:16:

_____

_____

_____

Did you notice that our light is equated to our good deeds? That's because they come from the same source; we have neither (light nor good deeds) without the Holy Spirit. What do our good deeds bring about according to this verse?

_____

Who gives the praise?

_____

Good works are just as much a part of God's predestined plan for us as anything else; we were created for them. They are not of ourselves, but God working through us by His Holy Spirit to show the world what a joyful, fulfilling, productive life looks like. It will not be without its struggles, but that's precisely where the light shines forth the brightest—when our efforts are hard but we persevere with joy.

The Holy Spirit imparts spiritual gifts to believers; by them we are enabled to carry out our divinely prepared good works (Ephesians 2:10). Paul confirms this in his letter to the Corinthians. Who does he state are given these gifts (manifestation of the Spirit), and for what reason (1 Corinthians 12:7)?

_____

Spiritual gifts, detailed in this chapter, provide the mode in which each believer will fulfill their distinct area of ministry. There are unique gifts for each individual person, put in and empowered by God (verses 12:4 and 6), to make Himself known. This letter to the Corinthians was written to a church dealing with serious issues. Divisiveness, immorality, and competing factions were prevalent among them; but their biggest issue was worldliness. Their jealousy, quarreling, and division were ruining the picture of Christ's bride.

Write 1 Corinthians 12:27.

_____.

Quite a bit of ink is used to enable us to understand that just as each part of the physical body is critical to its function and none are more or less important than another; so it is with the church. Paul's discourse concludes by telling the Corinthians to earnestly/eagerly desire the greater or higher gifts. What do you understand that to mean (1 Cor. 12:31a)?

_____

_____.

Spiritual gifts are for the benefit of the church; those that bring about the greatest benefit to others are the ones that are to be earnestly desired. Remember, this church was very worldly; they wanted the gifts that brought recognition to the exclusion of those that entailed quiet, behind the scenes service; these were not esteemed.

The problem was twofold: self-exaltation and distain for "lesser" gifts. As the one who provides the gifts, God knows what He's doing. He imparts talents and abilities according to His sovereign will for His grand purposes. As the recipients, our part is to use them well and do as Paul exhorts Timothy to do. What was his instruction regarding the gift of God in him (2 Timothy 1:6)?

_____.

God's glory is evident in the church when a group of people, diverse in every way imaginable, come together without envy or strife but in mutual purpose, contentedly utilizing their God-given uniqueness for the common good of the church. This is the picture we, the body of Christ, the bride, are to strive for; it is our purpose.

Our gifts are given and empowered by God, and any profitable result is to His credit and renown. However, that does not mean we can be passive, expecting God to work through us as though we're robots. We have to stir them up, like a fire, to keep them burning in full flame.

However, how does Paul conclude this verse (1 Corinthians 12:31b), with what words?

_____.

Bringing together our diverse gifts is imperative for the maturity and advancement of the church; Paul spends an entire chapter, emphasizing its importance. But there is a vital element that must be present; without it, no matter how extraordinary the gift or diligent the effort, it will be in vain.

According to 1 Corinthians 13:13, there is an excellent way. What is the virtue providing that way?

_____.

DAY 3

Love is the essence of the new covenant. This new covenant, written on our hearts, is reflected by a new attitude and a new strategy. I wonder which the Lord found more trying—inscribing the law on thick, hard tablets of stone with His finger or writing this new one on the unyielding, obstinate substance of our hearts!

Jesus makes an interesting statement in John 13:34. Write it here:

_____

_____

_____ .

How is this new—the command to love others was given back in the Old Testament? What does Jesus mean by this?

_____ .

The Greek word translated as *new* means "fresh, of a new kind." It's unprecedented, novel, uncommon, or unheard of. Clearly, Jesus doesn't mean loving others is a new concept, but the manner in which we are called to love is uncommon and altered. The key is found in the last part of the verse: "As I have loved you."
The Old Testament standard of love for others was to do them no harm. Based on Jesus's words, what is the New Testament standard?

_____ .

The standard of love, modeled by Jesus, is sacrificial. It's not characterized just by omitting harm, but by taking it a step farther and bringing about good toward others. The command is not new, but the scope of it is, going far beyond the borders previously set.

The new covenant Jesus brought can, at first glance, appear to be a walk in the park compared to the old covenant. But is it? You decide. Fill in the following:

The law said: **Jesus said:**

Do not kill.   (Matthew 5:22) _____

Do not commit adultery.   (Matthew 5:27–28) _____

Do not break an oath.   (Matthew 5:33–34) _____

An eye for an eye and a tooth for a tooth.   (Matthew 5:39–42) _____

Love your neighbor and hate your enemies.   (Matthew 5:44) _____

The new covenant is certainly straightforward, but easier? Not so much. The standard is much higher, which leads to a logical question. God's people were not able to live up to the standard of the old covenant, so why would (could) the new covenant requirement be greater?

_____

_____

_____.

Jesus sums up the new covenant in a couple of verses. In Matthew 7:12, He says this directive, "Sums up the Law and the Prophets." What does it instruct us to do?

_____.

When Jesus was asked what the most important commandment was, He said there was no greater commandment than these two. What are they (Mark 12:30–31)?

_____.

Lastly, how does Paul tell the church in Rome the law is fulfilled (Romans 13:8–10)?

_____.

Explain in your own words how love fulfills the law:

_____

_____.

God created humanity out of love. The great love chapter of 1 Corinthians 13, defining the characteristics of love, is displayed beautifully and wonderfully in God's actions toward us. If we follow these scriptures precisely, we can see it. It states love is not self-seeking; God did not keep His life and love to Himself but shared it by breathing life into man. He persevered in His love for selfish humanity and out of kindness, sent His Son: "For God so loved the world, that he gave his one and only Son." The evil He could not delight in, that enslaved man, turned to rejoicing in the truth of Jesus who, by His love, covered over a multitude of sin. He paid the penalty for the sin of mankind and keeps no record of wrongs. His love is patient, not desiring anyone to perish. He is always protecting: "I will never leave you or forsake you." It is always trusting that His suffering would bring many sons to glory and always hoping in confident assurance that those God has given to Christ will be with Him in His glory. His love never fails: "How priceless is your unfailing love!"

1 Corinthians 13 defines God's lofty standard for love. We tend to read it sentimentally, as the way things should be "in a perfect world." We consider it good advice rather than the expected measure we are to strive for. Remember, this was written to a church full of self-centered people in a determined attempt to cultivate Christ-like love in place of conceited, self-serving love. If that describes your church in any way (and it does, no matter who you are or where you attend), then its message applies.

Jesus displayed, as a model for us, the high standard of love; it was extravagant. Could you define your love for others this way? Let's narrow the field by qualifying "others" as just those in the church; your brothers and sisters (fellow body parts). Is it extravagant; meeting every criteria of 1 Corinthians 13? Why or why not?

_____

_____

_____.

The bride of Christ has to stop considering the all-inclusive, extreme love defined by this passage, as optional. It's not; it's commanded! It is without a doubt beyond our own ability; God alone possesses this type of unselfish love (agape). This is precisely why it's important. We have to allow Jesus to infuse His love into us so that we can pour it out on others so that the world may see and praise our great God.

The words used to describe love in 1 Corinthians 13 are not nouns but...you tell me, _____. This love is an action, not necessarily an affection; it's something we do but not necessarily something we feel. It's not that we never feel emotion; it's just not primary or even necessary. What we do, our actions toward God (pursuing Him through reading His Word, praying, seeking to please Him through obedience) and others, is more important and more telling than our words or feelings.

Our purpose as Christians is to give a right opinion of God to display Him to a world that doesn't know Him. If we just get along with those whom we have common interests or only love those who love us in return or only serve in areas that are fun or interesting, then we are in no way set apart from the masses.

Jesus addresses this attitude in Luke 6:32–36. Read these scriptures. What command does Jesus give in verse 35a that goes above and beyond our natural tendencies?

_____

_____.

What is Jesus's promise if we are obedient in verse 35b?

_____.

To be a "son of the Most High" is to reflect His image, representing Him in both name and nature. My son bears the name of his father; wherever he goes, he is associated with his dad. Not only that, but my son acts like his dad. They don't particularly resemble one another, so you wouldn't necessarily associate them by their looks, but it would not take you long to know who he belongs to by his actions, mannerisms and behaviors; the two of them couldn't be more alike. Likewise, people will see the God who is unseen in those who bear His name, Christians, and reveal His nature through actions and behavior.

How would you assess the quality of the image you're reflecting of God? What do people know of God by your actions, attitudes, and behaviors?

_____

_____

_____.

DAY 4 AND 5

Jesus brought a radical message during His earthly ministry, introducing an innovative way to live. The Sermon on the Mount expresses what Christ's kingdom is all about. This new strategy would set the church apart and change the world. Jesus's great sermon presented virtues for His bride to display so the world may see the love of the Bridegroom.

The Sermon on the Mount is detailed in the gospel of Matthew, chapters 5 through 7. We have already looked at a good bit of chapter 5 and viewed the high demands that go far beyond the apparent meaning of the words of the law: "You have heard that it was said . . . but I tell you." We'll concentrate on the eight paradoxical proclamations known as the Beatitudes (Matthew 5:3–10).

Read Matthew 5:1–12.

As we've done throughout this study, let's compare the meeting between God and His bride Israel as He gave her the conditions of their union, to this meeting between Jesus and His bride, as He lays out her course of action in preparation for their union in His kingdom.

- Both meetings were on a mountain
- The Lord God came down on Mount Sinai; the Lord Jesus went up the mountain.
- The Lord God spoke in thunder and lightning; the Lord Jesus in the voice of a man.
- The covenant at Mount Sinai consisted primarily of commandments of what not to do: "You shall not." The new covenant expressed in the Beatitudes is presented in a positive sense; virtues to employ that would lead to happiness and rewards.
- At Mount Sinai, the people were ordered to keep at a distance; on this mountain, all were invited to draw near to the presence of the Lord

In case you are like me and have always wondered where in the world this word *beatitude* came from, here it is. The word means "the blessing." It comes from the Latin word for *happy*, which was *beatus*, and the noun form *beatitudo*. This explains why some Bible translations say, "Blessed are those," and some say, "Happy are those." Unlike the common description of happy, which results from good fortune or favorable circumstances, blessed is not dependent on those things; it may be more aptly translated as "joyous or fully satisfied." The blessed person Jesus describes is not dependent on circumstances but is fully satisfied by the indwelling Spirit of God.

The beatitudes are a very familiar subject for most of us but do not allow that to cause you to dismiss their value in any way. They are critical, setting forth the characteristics Christ expects in His bride. They are virtues she must possess as evidence of her intentions, virtues that will make her joyful and fully satisfied.

From the beatitudes stated in Matthew 5:3–10, fill in the following chart (the first is provided):

Characteristic of One Fully Satisfied	The Reward
The poor in spirit	They will inherit the kingdom.

Now let's break them down one by one.

1. *The poor in Spirit possess the kingdom of heaven.* There are two words in the New Testament translated as "poor." One is *penes;* it means poor but able to help himself through his own labor. The other is *ptochos*, which is the word used here. It portrays a beggar, one who has nothing, destitute.

Why would *ptochos* be the more important distinction for the one who would possess the kingdom of heaven?

_____

_____

_____ .

The bride who is poor in spirit has come to Christ destitute, realizing she has nothing to offer that could acquire for her salvation from a holy God. She is a humble beggar, knowing that it is by His amazing grace alone that she is saved. Her financial status is not the issue; rich or poor, the attitude must be one that in spite of what she may or may not physically possess, only the righteousness of Christ will afford her the kingdom of heaven and that by humbly receiving it.

There is no question why this would be the first virtue Jesus gives, as it is foremost.

Read Luke 4:18 when Jesus reads the words of Isaiah in the synagogue proclaiming Himself to be the fulfillment of them. What does verse 18 say He was anointed to do?

_____ .

This is the same word we've been discussing; it represents the attitude of those Christ is seeking. The poor bring nothing to the table and are therefore grateful for the provision.

2. *Those who mourn or grieve are comforted.* Write in your own words what you believe it to mean that one who grieves is fully satisfied:

_____

_____

_____.

Realizing the bride price that Jesus paid for us, His bride, causes grief for the sin that made the cost so high. We mourn the fact that even still, we fall short of being the bride that He deserves because of lingering sin. The bride especially grieves over those rejecting the Bridegroom, who are not fully satisfied now nor will they enter His kingdom.

With those reasons in mind, how is she comforted in each of those ways?

_____

_____

_____.

Note: The word translated as grieve or mourn is generally defined as an inward attitude rather than an outward display. Why is that important?

_____

_____

_____.

3. *The meek inherit the earth.* Here is *The Complete Word Study New Testament* definition of *meekness*: "Meekness, expressed not in a man's outward behavior only nor in his relations to his fellow man or his mere natural disposition, but expressed rather as an inwrought grace of the soul, first and chiefly directed toward God. That attitude of spirit in which we accept God's dealings with us as good and do not dispute or resist."

This should disprove any negative concept you may have in your mind of meekness. Based on this definition and knowing this is a virtue Christ expects in His bride, how would you describe it? Give an example.

_____

_____

_____.

Like Christ, His bride should be full of passionate zeal; therefore, we know meekness cannot mean fearful or even passive. The bride is powerful beyond even her own understanding, but in humility she exhibits self-control, trusting God for the outcome of each and every situation. Obedience and submission, even to God, is counter to the culture, but they will bring about a fulfilled life; one that reflects God's kingdom.

4. *Those who hunger and thirst for righteousness will be filled.* It appears to me that the beatitudes are building blocks. If that's so, attaining the previous three brings about a deep desire for righteousness. I see this desire as two fold. How do you view it? What does it mean to crave righteousness?

_____

_____

_____.

The bride should naturally crave the righteousness that comes from God, an ever-increasing display of His imputed righteousness in her life. In addition, she longs for the righteousness to finally prevail over creation when the Bridegroom comes and makes all things new with no more corruption from sin. These are divine longings that God delights to fill.

Hunger and thirst are demanding needs that are detrimental to ignore. Would you say these appropriately characterize your desire and pursuit of righteousness? Why or why not?

_____

_____

_____

_____.

5. *The merciful will be shown mercy.* Mercy is not getting what you deserve; it's characterized by a caring attitude for those suffering in some way. What are some of the arenas in which we can be like Christ and show mercy (i.e., when someone is grieving or in habitual sin)?

_____

_____

_____.

On two occasions, Jesus told the Pharisees, "I desire mercy not sacrifice." The first occurred as Jesus was eating with "sinners" (Matthew 9:13), and the next when the hungry disciples picked wheat from the fields to eat on the Sabbath (Matthew 12:7). What was He telling them; what does it mean to desire mercy over sacrifice?

_____

_____

_____.

In both cases, Jesus was frustrated that the Pharisees had no compassion for those in their midst that were suffering in some way. The bride must be compassionate, showing the tender heart of Jesus to all those who cross her path, no matter why they may be in the situation they are in as this was our own plight when we received the mercy of God.

Write James's words on this subject (James 2:13c):

_____.

6. *The pure in heart will see God.* What does it mean to be pure in heart?

_____.

Oh, to have a heart completely free of impure or selfish motivation! One day. Until then, it is what we strive for, asking God continually to circumcise our hearts so that what we say and do is for His glory. And in that, we will see Him. Allowing God to use us without any desire or agenda of our own enables us to see His glory revealed. In talking about Christ's appearing, what does 1 John 3:3 say the bride will do in anticipation of that hope?

_____.

When our Bridegroom comes for us, we will want to have made ourselves pure! No bride would go to her wedding unclean; this is no different. This kind of purity/cleanliness cannot wait until the last minute (mainly because you don't know when that minute will be); we must be preparing.

7. *Peacemakers will be called sons of God.* The obvious application of a peacemaker applies here; we, the bride, should be people striving for the peace that comes from no conflict. The New Testament stresses the importance of living in peace with others. Write Romans 12:18:

_____.

Write Romans 14:19:

_____.

1 Peter 3:11 tells us we are to seek peace and pursue it. The emphasis is on personal effort. If we are to represent God appropriately, we cannot be striving against each other. Sometimes we need to just bless some things and let them go! Do it for the sake of Christ. Take a minute to consider anyone you are in conflict with, whether openly are just in the attitude of your heart. As far as it depends

on you, have you made every effort to make peace with that person? Do you even want to? Are you willing to obey Christ and be a peacemaker?

_____
_____
_____
_____.

There is another kind of peacemaker as well. What is it? Hint: Jesus is our peace (Ephesians 2:14) and the gospel of peace (Ephesians 6:15b).

_____.

The bride, at peace with God through the blood of Christ, now endeavors to be a peacemaker for others. Christ the Peacemaker has brought many sons to glory. We join His efforts as we present the gospel and intercede on behalf of those who don't know Him.

8. *Those who are persecuted because of righteousness receive the kingdom of heaven.* This one kind of makes you rethink number 4, doesn't it? But opposition is a normal mark of being a disciple; Jesus Himself warned that this would happen (John 15:20). But why is righteousness (not self-righteousness but Christ accredited righteousness) so offensive?

_____
_____.

For those who reject Christ, what "aroma" does 2 Corinthians 2:16 say Christians emit?

_____.

How do you respond to the smell of something dead?

_____.

The smell of death is repulsive; it causes people to turn away in disgust. This should serve to make us more understanding of the reaction Christians receive from unbelievers—we smell bad. I think the reason Jesus states that one can be happy or fully satisfied although persecuted is because it serves as evidence, a confirmation, that they are on track; they belong to Christ.

Jesus states in John 15:19 He has chosen His bride out of the world and set her apart. Because of that, how does the "world" respond?

_____.

More and more as time progresses, the world we live in will not be a welcome or comfortable place for the bride of Christ. But we can go beyond enduring hostilities; we can be happy because the kingdom of heaven is ours. What are the two virtues in the beatitudes that are rewarded with possession of the kingdom of heaven?

_____.

These are the "bookends" of the beatitudes, holding together all the virtues. It starts with a plea for grace that Jesus's righteousness would be imputed; it ends with a confirmation, via persecution, that indeed it was. Jesus says possessing the Beatitudes is the way to be happy, fully satisfied—blessed. You know, we use that term a lot—*blessed*. I enjoy hearing those who respond to inquiries of their well-being by saying, "I'm blessed," because it's true, and it serves as a great reminder to that truth. A Christian is the constant recipient of God's abundant blessings. But let's look at it from a different approach, as a personal assessment. Scripture says I'm blessed as I am humble, meek, compassionate, merciful, etc. From my end then, can I so quickly proclaim myself as blessed? I wear a little charm bracelet that says, "Completely Blessed." At this moment, I feel the need to take it off! I am completely blessed by the Lord, but is He completely blessed by me in that I convey the attributes He values? How beneficial it would be to use the term as not only a reminder of God's blessings but also as the standard of living set before us in which we will be blessed—the Beatitudes.

The Beatitudes must be given prominence as the challenging standard of living for the bride of Christ. They are so much more than a list of moral responsibilities, suggestions for nicer living. They represent a revolutionary strategy for living completely counter to human thought or nature. Their contrast is what makes them powerful. Based on the Beatitudes, what is to be our contrasting response in the face of the following?

Conflict?

_____.

Hatred?

_____.

Difficult people?

_____.

Offense?

_____.

Do you genuinely believe that taking this hard high road will make you happy and bring you greater satisfaction than striking back that your human nature demands? The answer is obvious. Because God has said it, we know intellectually that it must be true. But what can you do to make it a reality?

_____
_____
_____.

To live like this is to be meek; it is to trust that God's way, however contrary to our own, is good and pleasing and perfect. The Beatitudes are not suggestions; they are imperatives. Notice Jesus does not command them, not once.

That's because it's presupposed that, as the bride, they are presently held attributes that she strives to develop in ever-increasing measure knowing countercultural behavior will glorify God. By using compassion, mercy, humility, etc. as weapons rather than those the world would use displays true submission, trusting God for a good outcome. What kind of power does 2 Corinthians 10:4 say we can expect when using these weapons?

_____.

And what will God's power do?

_____.

To see a strategy work which is in complete contrast to common sense will cause people to wonder why; they can then be pointed to Christ. Revealing Christ and His love to others is our purpose, our calling; in this sense, the bride is also the matchmaker or marriage broker.

In Matthew 28, Jesus, true to the wedding analogy, is soon departing from His bride. As He returns to His Father's house to make preparations, He leaves her with parting words. Read Matthew 28:18–20 and state the three directives:

_____
_____
_____.

This Great Commission is the command of every Christian, but I think it's a mistake to interpret it as a stark directive, although that's how it reads. The charge from Jesus is not made from a negative attitude, feeling as though He's done all the hard work and is half mad about it so now it's time for us to pitch in.

Hebrews 12:2 makes it clear that Jesus endured the cross because of "the joy set before Him." What was that joy?

_____.

Just as the costly mission of Jesus for securing His bride was motivated by love, so shall our own mission be powered. Because the love of Christ dwells in our hearts through faith (Ephesians 3:17a), it has to be shared; the very nature of love is that it cannot be contained. We are to go and do likewise. Possessing His love, we reveal it and invite others into it. We are to receive this charge to tell the world about Christ, not from the standpoint that it's a necessary yet slightly unpleasant part of our duty but rather from the view of simply displaying the passion we have for the one we love and desiring that others know Him as well. This is what the disciples did, and it literally changed the world.

Iain Duguid defines Thomas Chalmer's message from "The Expulsive Power of a New Affection" as saying "Profound change in our behavior always comes from a change in what we love the most; not from external coercion." I believe this to hold true of our obedience to the Great Commission; our achievements will be greatly limited when motivated only externally. However, when we love Christ with all our hearts, soul, minds, and strength, we cannot stop from telling others; it pours out. 2 Corinthians 5:14 confirms this. What is the compelling or controlling force at work in us?

_____.

According to the next verse (15), what are we to be compelled to do?

_____.

The love that Jesus expresses toward us and imparts to us should affect every area of our lives. Loving God and loving others fulfill all other commands and identify believers as belonging to Christ. Love is distorted in our culture; loyal, enduring and unselfish love is often substituted for a cheap version of mere emotion and physical satisfaction. Christians have a unique opportunity to display the genuine love of Jesus to those who desperately need it. But we also need to show it in abundance to each other in the body of Christ—we need it too! Without it, we have nothing.

When Jesus was asked about signs indicating His return, He gave an extensive list. According to Matthew 24:12, what was one of those signs?

_____.

This is completely unacceptable for us, the bride! What an appalling thought that the Bridegroom, who has paid so dearly for His bride and is currently at work preparing a place for her, would return to find her cold, indifferent and unconcerned. Jesus said this *will* happen so we must be on guard and alert to any arena that might draw our affections away from Jesus.

Read Titus 2:11–14. These verses teach that we are learning how to do some things and how not to do others. We are growing in grace as we anticipate something. What is it (verse 13)?

_____.

He is coming!

"I saw heaven standing open and there before me was a white horse, whose rider is called Faithful and True. His eyes are like blazing fire, and on his head are many crowns. He has a name written on him that no one knows but he himself. He is dressed in a robe dipped in blood, and his name is the Word of God. On his robe and on his thigh he has this name written: KING OF KINGS AND LORD OF LORDS" (Revelation 19:11–13 and 16).

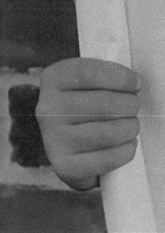

DAY 1

The current timeline on God's kingdom calendar finds us, the bride of Christ, physically separated from our Bridegroom. Jesus has returned to His Father's house to prepare a place for us (John 14:2), and we are left with our own preparations to make. Anxious to be together, this time can seem endless.

Long-distance romances are a challenge, especially in the days before cell phones and computers. In those days, letters were the mode of communication. What might you expect a letter from the bridegroom to his bride to contain? Surely, they would include a confirmation of his love, assurance of his return, encouragement, and direction for his imminent arrival. Consider for a minute what a treasure these letters would be to the bride. Can you see her tenderly removing them from their place of safekeeping? The letters are creased and worn from folding and unfolding as she reads them again and again; this is all she has of her beloved, for now.

During our separation, we, the bride, have letters from Jesus—letters to treasure and know by heart, letters to prepare us for His return. According to Revelation 1:4, who is the book of Revelation addressed to?

_____.

In studying Revelation, what are the three means of blessings according to Revelation 1:3?

_____.

What is the implication of the last part of the above verse as well as Revelation 1:1?

_____.

The truth that Jesus is coming soon gives a sense of urgency to the reading, understanding, and implementation of His words. The entire book of Revelation, not just the letters represented in chapters 2 and 3, is written to the church and is meant to be read and taken to heart. Unfortunately, time will only permit us to concentrate on the messages to the seven specific churches.

The church is the means God uses to proclaim His truth and presence in the world. She is His instrument for accomplishing the final phase of His great plan as His presence is powerfully at work in and through her. Although other churches existed at the time of this revelation, the seven referred to exclusively seem to represent the church as a whole.

This book is a revelation; an uncovering or unveiling. It was not written to satisfy the curiosity of the readers regarding future events but to bring encouragement and hope. The church was facing trials and persecution; these would continue to afflict the church. Jesus Christ is the divine author of the book and revealer of the events leading up to His final victory when all evil is defeated and His kingdom is established on earth. The church, portrayed as "overcomers" throughout Revelation, has reason to persevere as Jesus's letter visibly discloses that He, the Bridegroom, will come for His bride, the church, to live together in intimate communion: "Now we see but a poor reflection as in a mirror; *then* we shall see face to face. Now I know in part; *then* I shall know fully, even as I am fully known" (1 Corinthians 13:12, italics mine).

The events presented in Revelation are very sobering. Jesus's second coming will bring about the last judgment; there will be no more second chances, no opportunity to change sides. The bride must be ready. Therefore, before any message of judgment on the unbelieving world is presented, it is the church He takes to task.

Where does 1 Peter 4:17 say God's judgment, His chastening and purifying work, will begin?

_____ .

The church, Christ's bride, must accurately express Christ's truth and righteousness in order to influence the world; therefore, judgment must begin with the house of God. While the appeals of the letters are personal to the local church they speak to, the principles dealt with are universal in nature. In other words, the messages are for us.

Of the seven messages, each and every one, without fail, contains a particular exhortation. What is it (Revelation 2:7, 11, 17, 29, 3:6, 13, 22)?

_____ .

Right now, take your hands and reach to both sides of your head. Did you find ears there? Great, this is talking to you! Now that we've settled that, the next instruction is to *hear*. This word infers more than just receiving words; it assumes action to those words. It's not enough to just hear and acknowledge them; they must be put into practice.

How is the person who only hears described in James 1:22?

_____.

These are important words, and we want to glean from them all that we can since it is individual believers who comprise the church. The health and well-being of the church is the personal responsibility of each of us, not just the leaders. Note that all the letters were to be read to all the churches; it is one letter to seven churches. The commendations and rebukes were to be applied to each church as well as to the church today.

We begin with the church in Ephesus. Read Revelation 2:1–7.

We will see as we continue to study these churches, that Christ is represented differently in each letter with each description being tied to the problem of that particular church.

The message begins by telling us who's speaking. We know it to be Jesus.

How is He depicted?

_____.

The previous verse (Revelation 1:20) informs us that the seven stars are the "angels" of the church. Most scholars agree that these are the ministers, elders, or leaders of the church, not an angel since angels are never leaders in a church. The seven golden lampstands are the churches themselves.

Did you notice the verbs used: *holds* and *walks*? What is He holding? Where is He walking? What does that mean?

_____

_____.

Jesus is the one with authority over the church and its leaders and is intimately involved in their workings. Paul, Timothy, and John all served this particular church. In fact, John wrote his gospel and three epistles there. It was a privileged church to have experienced such prominent leaders.

Ephesus was a large and prosperous city with four great trade roads making it known as the gateway to Asia. It held one of the seven wonders of the ancient world, the Temple of Diana (Artemis in Greek). The temple employed thousands of priests and priestesses and lent to the major industry of manufacturing images of this goddess. Ephesus was a city known for its idolatry.

For what does Jesus commend this church (verses 2–3 and 6)?

_____

_____

_____

_____.

In spite of their pagan surroundings and the prevalence of false teaching, the Ephesian church stood true to their faith for the sake of Christ's name without becoming weary. Could the same commendation be given to us? We certainly find ourselves in similar surroundings. The city I live in is very prosperous (and certainly large), causing easy distractions from the purposes of Christ. Not to stretch a point, but my city (and perhaps yours as well) certainly has its own magnificent "temples" to other gods, just not as blatant. Three separate impressive skylines display wealth and ability; there's nothing wrong with these until they become our god. Evil thrives here in countless ways, operating in our city is the largest abortion "supercenter" in the nation, as well as rampant sex trade industries.

And just as in Ephesus, false teachings are alarmingly common. Philosophies, principles and ideas that are far from the biblical standard are presented as truth and readily available.

What message does Jesus want to speak to you regarding your worship of Him alone? Are you doing His work, making sacrifices (physical, financial, emotional) for the sake of His name? Is your definition of evil the same as Christ's, and are you standing against it in your own life as well as in the community? Are you familiar enough with His Word to enable you to see a false doctrine when presented? Take the time now to let the Holy Spirit speak to you. For those areas which you are doing well, hear His voice of encouragement as you persevere. But also allow Him to convict you of the areas that need attention. Write any thoughts, prayers, confessions here:

_____

_____

_____

_____.

The Ephesians were doing many things well. However, what does Jesus hold against them (verse 4)?

_____.

The major translations use the words _left_, _abandoned_ or _forsaken_. What is not used is _lost_. Although the Ephesian church had earlier been commended by Paul for their love (Ephesians 1:15), they had become careless in their affections. They had not heeded Jesus's warning that the love of most would grow cold and been on guard. How is it that we, as the hymn states so well, are so prone to wander from God, leaving the God we love?

What was the church exhorted to do (Revelation 2:5a)?

_____.

Any relationship, especially a marriage, takes work. Negligence will reduce the union that was once passionate and exciting to apathetic coexistence. A marriage counselor would instruct a couple in this situation to start "dating" again, carve out intimate time together, enjoy each other again—in other words, "do the things you did at first."

How are you guarding your relationship with Jesus? Are you doing the things that will keep it vibrant and intimate? What are they?

_____

_____

_____.

Abandoning the love we first had for Jesus is dangerous; it leads to rote religion, just what the Pharisees were guilty of. Based on this scripture, it is sin; otherwise, why would we be told to repent? If your love has become cold, confess that to Him. He already knows; He's just waiting for you to acknowledge it.

Our words, abilities, work, and sacrifices are all in vain. They count for nothing, apart from love. If we learned anything last week, it was the significance of love, specifically the love *for* Christ that produces the love *of* Christ. To be fruitful, God glorifying people, we have to stay connected to the vine that is Christ. Apart from Him, we can do nothing.

What was the warning given to this church (Revelation 2:5b)?

_____.

Spurgeon states, "A church has no reason for being a church when she has no love within her heart or when that love grows cold. Lose love, lose all." We all know of churches that are nothing more than social clubs, mere organizations, in which the glory of the Lord is not present. Although it takes an enormous amount of work in a variety of arenas for a church to exist, careful attention should be paid to our motivation and focus, which is love for Christ and the desire to bring glory to His name. The glory of God is to shine brightly in the church. As the light of individual believers come together to make up the church, we must each be aware of and take responsibility for the condition of our own light. Even one nonexistent or flickering flame diminishes the intensity of the light the church is to provide to the world. As we collectively bring forth the light endowed to us, the light shines bright for all to see, like a city on a hill (Matthew 5:14).

Here's an interesting note: The lampstand, referring back to Exodus 25:31–36, is made of one piece—just as Christ is one with His church (Ephesians1:22–23). It had six branches—six being the number of man—plus the main shaft to equal seven, the number of completion. It exists as a symbol showing that man is *only* complete in Christ (John 15:5, Revelation 1:13)

A reward is promised to those who overcome. Based on the warning, what is it we must overcome and keep overcoming (Revelation 2:7)?

_____.

As we overcome, what is the promise (Revelation 2:7)?

_____.

This letter began with Christ's identification as the one with authority over and intimate involvement with His church. He has both the power and the awareness necessary to grant the promise of eternal life: "The Lord knows those who are His" (2 Timothy 2:19). We have great incentive to keep moving forward in our love for Christ and the work resulting from that love.

What does Romans 8:18 say regarding suffering we are called to endure for His sake?

_____.

The glory of God in us reveals Jesus to a lost world as the hope of glory fixes our eyes on Christ as our bridegroom and the eternal union we will share with Him.

DAY 2

The second message is to the church in Smyrna. Read Revelation 2:8–11.
How does Jesus address Himself to this church (Revelation 2:8b)?

_____.

Smyrna was a beautiful and prosperous city where emperor worship was a matter of great pride and loyalty among the people. The uncompromising church in Smyrna stood in contrast to the deification of Rome and its emperors. This church is one of only two that receive no rebuke from Christ, only commendations.

What does Christ "know" about them (verses 9–10)?

_____.

Standing for Christ had cost these Christians dearly, affecting their livelihood. Because they would not compromise their beliefs and call Caesar "lord," they were excluded from guilds, which resulted in unemployment and poverty.

The Jewish population in this city was particularly anti-Christian; they slandered the believers as heretics and agitators. They were the same ones who demanded the martyrdom of Polycarp and others.

Tradition states that Polycarp was personally discipled by the apostle John and served as bishop of the church in Smyrna. When he was eighty-six years old, he was arrested on charges of being a Christian. Christianity was considered a politically dangerous cult due to its rapid growth. Polycarp had a gentle nature and was a dearly loved. Because of this, even the arresting officers urged him to testify that Caesar is lord and offer a pinch of incense to Caesar's statue so that he could escape torture and death. Polycarp's response to this was, "Eighty-six years I have served Christ, and He never did me any wrong. How can I blaspheme my King who saved me?" The soldiers were then ordered to nail him to a stake to be burned alive. Polycarp stopped them, saying, "Leave me as I am. For He who grants me to endure the fire will enable me also to remain on the pyre unmoved, without the security you desire from nails." The fire was lit, and Polycarp died a martyr for his faith in Jesus. This was the degree of persecution the church in Smyrna was enduring. This was the church Jesus instructs not to be afraid!

In verse 10, the Lord tells them not to be afraid of what they are _____ to suffer. He tells them up front so they needn't be afraid; God is in control. Just as Jesus told Peter that Satan had sought permission to sift him, He now relays a similar scenario to this church. Satan would be behind the action when some of them were put into _____. He tells them they will suffer persecution for _____.

This may not necessarily mean ten actual days; the point is (1) they will suffer and 2) there will be a beginning and an end to it.

How would you respond if this letter came to your church? Would you more likely seek a place of refuge from the oncoming suffering or dig in for a firm place to stand during the onslaught?

_____

_____

_____

It's a heavy question, I know, and nearly impossible for us Western Christians to have to answer. We really have no point of reference that would enable us to comprehend what it would be like to risk all we have for Christ. Our biggest concerns are along the line of public embarrassment or social rejection. What could we know about laying down our lives for the gospel? But the blood of martyrs has been called "the seeds of the church."

"The church at Smyrna grew into one of the most revered and influential churches of its time because its leaders were willing to lay down their live for Christ and the gospel" (*Revelation: Unlocking the Future*, Edward Hindson).

Historically, persecution has always caused increase in the church, both numerically and spiritually. Why would that be true?

_____

_____

_____

This is another example of the heresy of the prosperity gospel. We are never made strong by indulgence, not in our physical lives and not in our spiritual lives. The church, as a body and as individuals, is strengthened through resistance. We're proven genuine by fire (1 Peter 1:7).

What is the church exhorted to do, and what will they receive according to the latter part of verse 10?

_____

A willingness to sacrifice your life for the cause of Christ reveals a genuine belief; you wouldn't die for a lie. It also reveals an understanding of our real citizenship. This life is a breath, a vapor. The saying, "You only live once" may be tragically true for some; but for those in Christ, this life is merely a means to an end, an end worth striving and sacrificing for—eternity with God.

What are the overcomers promised (verse 11b)?

_____.

I would not want to presume what everyone reading this understands "the second death" to mean. There's a little saying that goes like this: "Born twice, die once; born once, die twice." We are born into this world physically with a sin nature; we must be born again in Christ to live in His righteousness, no longer slaves to sin. We will eventually die a physical death, but being united with Christ, we will live a new and eternal life with Him. If we are born only once—physically—then we will die twice. The first death is physical; the second is the death sentence of eternal damnation given at the judgment seat of Christ for those He never knew because they were separated from Him by sin.

We should remember that overcoming doesn't always mean surviving. Meeting death through the cause of Christ is not defeat; it's overcoming! The one who is the first and the last, who died and came to life again, has gone before us. (He's been there, done that!) Whether we are facing death or in the valley of the shadow of death, we need not fear. Death has no power, no "sting."

How does 2 Corinthians 2:14 say God always leads us?

_____.

Jesus Christ Himself will place the victor's crown on the head of His triumphant bride.

The next church in the progression is in Pergamum. Read Revelation 2:12–17.

Pergamum was an impressive city built on a hill one thousand feet above the surrounding countryside, creating a natural fortress. This sophisticated city was the center of Greek culture and education. It was also the center of Roman power and authority. Pergamum was the site of the first temple of the Caesar-cult, erected in honor of Augustus Caesar, leading to a predominance of the cult of Caesar worship. The city also had a temple dedicated to the god of healing, Asclepius, whose insignia is still a medical symbol today—the entwined serpent on a staff. In addition, it had temples to numerous Greek and Roman gods, including an altar to Zeus—the god of power. This immense open-air structure stood near the summit of the acropolis, a truly impressive sight.

Note: The altar from the temple of Zeus found its way to Berlin. It went on display in the Pergamum Museum in 1930 "just in time to inspire one of the most brutal dictators the world has ever seen" (*The Seat of Satan: Ancient Pergamum*, by Gordon Robertson), Adolf Hitler, who reportedly often visited the exhibit. In fact, he was so obsessed with it, he insisted it be used as the model in constructing the platform for his Nazi rallies.

As you can see, Pergamum was a center for idolatry. Caesar claimed to be god and acknowledgement and worship of his deity was demanded from the people. Declaring yourself a Christian and worshipper of the one true God and Savior, Jesus Christ, in this city was going to provoke a great deal of hostility. The governor of Pergamum had the right to judge guilt or innocence. He had also been given the rare authority to perform executions. This was known as "the right of the sword." If a Christian refused to acknowledge Caesar as god, the governor could put that person to death by the sword.

What description of Himself does Jesus give to this church (verse 12)?

_____ .

The Christian citizens in Pergamum lived under its domineering idolatrous rule symbolized by the sword. But their citizenship was of another kingdom whose Ruler's sharp, doubled-edged sword brings greater fear as it represents His ultimate authority and judgment. Luke 12:4–5 says, "I tell you, my friends, do not be afraid of those who kill the body and after that can do no more. But I will show you whom you should fear: Fear him who, after killing the body, has power to throw you into hell."

Since most of us don't face the sword of death, what threats tempt you to please man instead of God?

_____

_____ .

Jesus assures this church in verse 13a, that He _____ where they live.

Jesus acknowledged the fear and hostility they endured by living in such a difficult environment where Satan lived and ruled through its rampant idolatry. What did He commend them for (verse 13)?

_____

_____ .

Pergamum stayed true to the name of Christ "even in the days of Antipas my faithful witness." Antipas was probably the bishop or pastor of the church. Tradition holds that he was martyred, slow roasted, inside a hollow brass bull designed for human sacrifices that stood at the top of the altar of Zeus.

Rick Renner, in his book *A Light in the Darkness*, describes the method of execution suffered by Antipas: "They would take the victim, place him inside the bull, and they would tie him in such a way that his head would go into the head of the bull. Then they would light a huge fire under the bull, and as the fire heated the bronze, the person inside of the bull would slowly begin to roast to death. As the victim would begin to moan and to cry out in pain, his cries would echo through the pipes in the head of the bull so it seemed to make the bull come alive."

Jesus honors this hero of the faith by calling him a "faithful witness," which is interestingly the designation given to Christ in Revelation 1:5 and 3:14. The word *martyr* comes from the Greek word for *witness*. Jesus is the faithful witness of the truth from God, who sent Him to earth do die for sins. Satan seeks to destroy loyalty to Christ by persecution, but the deaths of His faithful witnesses, martyrs, serves to strengthen the church.

Nevertheless, this church had a few things against them. What were they (verse 14–15)?

_____

_____.

Although the church stood strong against persecution, they were compromising in dangerous areas. What Satan was unable to do from the outside as a roaring lion seeking to devour (1 Peter 5:8), he was accomplishing from the inside as the deceiving serpent (Revelation 12:9).

What was the teaching of Balaam according to Revelation 2:14?

_____.

The story of Balaam is found in Numbers 22–25. Since we won't have the time to go into great detail here, it would be an interesting and beneficial topic to explore on your own (especially since it involves a talking donkey).

Jesus also addressed the teaching of the Nicolaitans, which, as we saw in His words to the church of Ephesus, He hates. "This teaching is believed to have derived from Nicolas of Antioch, whose disciples insisted that Christian freedom means 'lawlessness'" (*The Book of Revelation: Unlocking the Future*, Edward Hindson).

The false doctrine represented in these two teachings is summed up as immorality and idolatry. Those that were holding to these teachings were using Christian liberty to justify their participation in worldly activities. They saw no harm in a little idolatry, a little immorality, a little compromise of the truth. What would it hurt? In fact, making some concessions could actually ease the hostility toward them. They sought to coexist as painlessly as possible, as well as enjoy the sinful pleasures of their society.

What temptation are you finding hard to stand against? Do you feel the pull to be open-minded and tolerant of practices and attitudes that the Bible clearly speaks against? Are there areas of compromise that seem harmless?

_____

_____

_____ .

How do you balance separating yourself from sin while still building relationships with sinners?

_____

_____

_____

_____ .

What warning does this church receive (verse 16)?

_____

_____ .

Hebrews 4:12 states God's Word is _____ than a double-edged sword. It penetrates even to _____ soul and spirit, joints and marrow; it _____ the thoughts and attitudes of the heart.

The church is called to repent; both those following the false teaching as well as those who were allowing them to continue. If not, Jesus will use His sharp double-edged sword to make some separations and confront them with His word. His judgments against them will prove right in the light of His truth as opposed to the deception of their doctrine.

What does Jesus promise the overcomers (verse 17)?

_____

_____ .

Overcomers are those who prevail over compromise and the temptation to be part of the world; they are in it but not of it. Hidden manna suggests the spiritual nourishment that faithful believers receive for keeping the church doctrinally pure. By refusing the offerings of pagan gods but choosing instead to feast on the bread from heaven (John 6:51), they receive the manna now and at the banquet of Christ and His bride.

The white stone referred to may be alluding to the stones given to a winning athlete as an admission pass to the victory celebration. It could also indicate the stones given as an invitation to a banquet or feast. And it may be in reference to the white stone used by a judge to cast a verdict of innocence for a person on trial. These would all apply in a spiritual sense to the believer.

Read Isaiah 62:2 and write the last part of the verse:

_____.

Many times in Scripture, a person is given a new name by the Lord, indicating action on His part to change the status or character of that person—i.e., Abram/Abraham, Sarai/Sarah, Saul/Paul. We will each receive a new name that signifies our change in status (from unredeemed to redeemed) and character (sinner to saint). God's transforming grace makes us new and different from who we once were. The Lord's new name for us will reflect depth of intimacy as only you and He will know it.

DAY 3

Traveling east is the Church of Thyatira. Read Revelation 2:18–29.

Thyatira was a small city, but it receives the longest message. It was a military town and commercial center with many trade guilds. The guilds played an important role politically, socially, economically, and religiously. Each had their own patron deity, feasts, and seasonal festivities that included sexual revelries. The domination of these guilds placed Christians living there in a terrible position; they could either participate which would put them in opposition to the church, or they could refuse to be associated with them, which would mean that they could not make a living.

Some commentators state that the thriving cloth industry in the city, where weaving, dyeing, and sewing were the major sources of income, generated a number of powerful and wealthy woman who dominated the trade guilds. Lydia, who became a believer, was one such woman.

Read Acts 16:14. What was Lydia's occupation, and where was she from?

_____.

Unlike the other cities where cult worship was prominent, this city was unimportant religiously; it had taken a backseat to commercial enterprise. Thyatira did, however, have a special temple to Apollo, the sun god. Caesar, who was worshipped there, was considered the reincarnation of Apollo and called by his followers "the son of God."

How does Jesus address Himself to this church (verse 18)?

_____.

Jesus identifies Himself, not Apollo or Caesar, as the true Son of God. The description of the living Christ walking among the churches with eyes of blazing fire is in stark contrast to the immobile Apollo, whose eyes, instead of glowing, are dead, made of stone.

What commendations did this church receive (verse 19)?

_____

_____.

For what were they rebuked (verse 20)?

_____.

If you could combine the church in Ephesus with this church, you'd have a winner. Ephesus was weak in love, love for God and others, but they held a strong line against false teachers. Thyatira, on the other hand, excelled in love, persevering and serving Christ, and others and apparently doing it in an increasing capacity. But they tolerated false teaching.

The culture in Thyatira produced strong, independent women (Lydia). However, strength and independence was misused by Jezebel to defy God's authority and direction for the church. Jezebel most likely refers to a woman/women of influence in the church who was corrupting the believers with false teaching. Jesus points out that this woman "calls herself" a prophetess. While the Bible gives examples of women who've received the gift of prophecy from the Holy Spirit (Luke 2:36, Acts 21:9, 1 Corinthians 11:5), this was not the case with her; she was self-ordained. She must have possessed some unique gifts since obviously she had been given a place of authority and many in the church were following her teaching. But her ideas were contrary to God's Word, following closely to those of Balaam and the Nicolaitans. She was able to convince believers to compromise with the Roman religion and the practices of the guilds so that Christians would not lose their jobs or their lives. But in the end, they would lose a lot more.

Jesus speaks of the calamity that will be coming to her and her followers. What reason is given for these disasters (verses 21 and 22)?

_____.

Jezebel and her supporters would suffer intensely because of their unrepentance! For all of us, even grievous sins can be forgiven if we repent. God is faithful and just to forgive those who repent and cleanse them from all unrighteousness (1 John 1:9).

What reason does He give in verse 23 for striking her children dead?

_____

_____.

Note: the "children" likely refer to the followers of the Jezebel's teaching and not necessarily natural children.

Jesus will use this church as an example. The blazing eyes of the Son of God sees through all falsehood, deception, and misrepresentation while His feet of bronze move through His church to exercise judgment on it.

Write the first several words of verse 24:

_____.

Picture yourself in a room with the fellow believers of your church listening to these messages. The reader delivers Jesus's scathing words of anger and judgment, then pauses. He takes a breath… and says, "Now for the rest of you." What would be going through your mind? I would be so frightened about what might be coming next!

What does Jesus say to those who had not been misled (verses 24–25)?

_____.

The church at Thyatira that was doing so well apart from "that woman" would receive no other burden or reprimand beyond ridding her from their midst. Holding on to what they had, wisdom and discernment, would keep them on the right path and guard against a reoccurrence.

Believers should never take a light view of heresy of any kind; it destroys people for eternity. Paul warned Timothy of a day coming when people would not tolerate sound doctrine. What would they demand instead (2 Timothy 4:3b–4)?

_____.

I can think of several heresies that are predominant in our culture and even the church—i.e., prosperity gospel and many roads to God. What religious heresies do you believe the church should be most on guard against?

_____
_____
_____.

What two things are overcomers promised (verses 26 and 28)?

_____.

What description is Jesus given in Revelation 22:16d?

_____.

What hopeful words to encourage perseverance! Jesus Christ, the Morning Star, rises over the darkness, and His bride, the church, reigns with Him in authority, justice and mercy.

Those who have ears, hear what the Spirit says. "This is a letter that applies to everyone. It applies to those who are like Jezebel, who lead others into sin. It applies to those who follow the teaching of a Jezebel, and follow others into sin. It applies to those who permit a Jezebel to work her wickedness. And it applies to the faithful who must hold fast" (blueletterbible.com, David Guzik).

The next church on our journey is the church of Sardis. Read Revelation 3:1–6.

Sardis was positioned on a natural acropolis about 1,500 feet above the main roads. Its vertical rock walls that formed a nearly impregnable fortress made it a militarily strategic city. It was the capital of Lydia and one of the greatest cities in the ancient world. This city was named necropolis of "a thousand hills" because of the hundreds of burial mounds visible from Sardis.

Since it lay at the junction of five major roads, it was an important city of trade, boasting a thriving woolen industry. Although the wealth of the city still afforded its people a luxurious lifestyle, it was in decline, a shadow of its former splendor. This appeared to be the problem in the church as well. The peace and economic prosperity they were enjoying had led them into complacency and moral decadence.

How does Jesus identify Himself (verse 1b)?

_____ .

The seven spirits of God, or sevenfold Spirit, is the Holy Spirit. Who are the seven stars according to Revelation 1:20?

_____ .

This church faced none of the opposition present in the others, which would lead us to believe it must be flourishing, but it seems the lack of conflict was having the opposite effect. This church was lazy and apathetic, giving them the distinction of being the first church to receive no commendations from Christ.

Jesus says, "I know your deeds." How does He finish that statement (verse 1c)?

_____

_____ .

At one time, Sardis had obviously been a healthy, prosperous church because they had made a name for themselves; but they were alive in name only, living on past glories. In truth, they were lifeless. George Eldon Ladd defined the church in Sardis as "a picture of nominal Christianity, outwardly prosperous, busy with the externals of religious activity, but devoid of spiritual life and power" (*A Commentary on the Revelation of John*). This sounds very similar to Paul's description of people in the last days as "having a form of godliness but denying its power" (2 Timothy 3:5).

What is this church told to do (verse 2)?

_____

_____ .

Jesus's emphatic plea to wake up is a word that means watch, give strict attention to, and take heed, lest through remission and indolence some destructive calamity suddenly overtake one. This would have gotten their attention as historically Sardis's overconfidence and complacency had led to its ruin.

One of the accounts is of Croesus, a Lydian king. While under siege by Cyrus the Persian, he had fortified himself in the acropolis of Sardis, and because of its position, Cyrus could not capture him. But the Persians remained watchful and one afternoon, a Persian soldier witnessed a Lydian soldier climb down the back of the wall of Sardis to retrieve his fallen helmet. That night, Cyrus's army snuck up that path, surprising the Lydian army, and conquered the city. Croesus and his people, assured of their security, had become lazy rather than watchful. The watchmen on the walls had not seen the enemy scaling the cliffs, and they paid for that mistake with their lives.

Read Isaiah 62:6–7 (Come on and do it, you won't be sorry).

Whose "walls" has God placed you as a watchman over? Could it be a rebellious child, an unsaved loved one, a persecuted church, a person enslaved by some sin, or someone indifferent, uninterested, and apathetic toward the Lord? Unquestionably, we are to be the watchmen over our own lives and the livelihood of our church.

Picture yourself as a watchman high on a tower. You're alone at your post, and in the darkness, you spot the enemy, with evil intent, scaling the wall. What will you do? We have the unbelievable advantage of calling on the Lord of Hosts, the God of angel armies! It is both a benefit *and* responsibility.

What are those who call on the Lord told to do (Isaiah 62:6c)?

_____ .

What else are they directed to do (verse 7a—this is awesome!)?

_____ .

I love this verse so much! We not only have permission, we are actually instructed not to give the Lord even a moment of peace until He establishes that in which we are striving in prayer. (Just to be cautious, let me remind you that our endeavors must be according to His will; in His Name.)

A healthy, fruitful church demands that its members be alert and watchful. We have enemies of our faith—one of the most deadly being apathy.

Where is apathy most prominently displayed in the universal church? Are there areas in which your own church appears apathetic? How much responsibility do individual members of the church have in causing apathy and destroying it?

_____

_____

_____

_____.

The church must never become satisfied with its status in the community, usefulness to Christ's cause or knowledge and exaltation of God's Word. And the church, as a body, will only be as strong as its members. Each individual member must make a commitment to progress in their knowledge of Christ through His Word in order to cultivate an ever-increasing conformity to His image. To become satisfied with the status quo is to fall into the same sin as this church, alive only by reputation.

Have you ever rested in your reputation? For instance, perhaps you were once a powerful prayer warrior, but in all honesty, it's no longer true. But you let your reputation of what was once true stand by allowing others to believe it rather than correcting its inaccuracy. Spiritually speaking, what do you have a reputation for, and is it consistent with your life?

_____

_____

_____

_____.

The church at Sardis must have been an active church because by the looks of it, it appeared alive. Jesus doesn't accuse them of no deeds. What does He charge them with (verse 2b)?

_____.

The word *complete* means to make full, to fill up, to fill to the full, to be rendered full. With this definition in mind, what were their deeds hollow of?

_____.

Activity does not imply life. Jesus identified Himself to this church as holder and possessor of the fullness of the church and the Holy Spirit. Life and fullness is found in Him alone. Our efforts done apart from the Holy Spirit are meaningless and fruitless; they're dead.

Jesus is famous for giving life to the dead. He has the ability and desire to resurrect this church, but some things will be required of them. What are they (verse 3)?

_____

_____.

The directive was not just to remember but to exercise that memory. What had they received?

_____.

What had they heard?

_____.

The church had received the Holy Spirit living in them as well as the living and active word of God, everything they needed for obedience. In the opening chapter of Revelation, how does Jesus identify Himself to John (Revelation 1:18a)?

_____.

The one aspect of Christianity that sets it apart from other religions is the fact that our Savior is alive and He has given His bride life in His name. Therefore, the church, the representation of Christ's body through which He speaks and acts, that is lifeless, is an appalling offense. No wonder Christ demanded repentance for this horrible distortion of His name.

Apparently, churches and individual believers can be dead without it being easily noticed. Obviously, the presence of the Holy Spirit is missing from a dead church. What would be some of the characteristics of a dead or dying church? Example, man's agenda over God's, church growth over spiritual growth, glorification of self rather than God.

_____

_____

_____

_____.

What preventative measures should you take to avoid your or your church's slow death?

_____.

The life of Christ must be reflected in His church both individually and corporately; otherwise, He will come with stealth and destruction, much like the past enemies of the city of Sardis had.

Fortunately, there was a small remnant in the church that had remained steadfast in their commitment to live for Christ. What is Jesus's promise to them and all who overcome (verse 5–6)?

_____

_____.

This message is all about our "name," reminiscent of the promise to the overcomers in Pergamum who receive a new name. The Greek word for *name* is *onoma*; it's used four times in these six verse:

1. "You have a *name* for being alive" (verse 1).
2. "Yet you have a few *names*" (verse 4).
3. "I will never blot out his *name*" (verse 5).
4. "But will acknowledge his *name*" (verse 5).

The authenticity of our name will be brought to light. As we bear Christ's name, we have to diligently guard our reputations, being watchful over any and every enemy that seeks to destroy it, whether through sin or apathy.

DAY 4

The sixth message is to the church of Philadelphia. Read Revelation 3:7–13.

In contrast to the church in Sardis, who received no commendations but only rebuke, the church of Philadelphia receives no admonishments, just praise. The city was strategically situated on a main highway which led from Europe to the East, giving it the designation of being "the gateway to the East" and a place of tremendous opportunity. Because of the many temples in Philadelphia, it was also known as little Athens. As advantageous as the location was, the city had a major problem because it was located on a geological fault and under constant threat of earthquakes.

How does Jesus identify Himself to the church (verse 7)?

_____

_____.

Holy and true Jesus is set apart from sin, absolutely pure and perfect in action, word, character, and purpose. He is the genuine, authentic one true God; the opposite of that which is fictitious or counterfeit. He is true in what He says and true in who He is.

And He holds the key of David: Christ possesses the power and authority to lock and unlock the door, admit or exclude entrance, into the kingdom of God. Access to God's kingdom is through Christ alone (John 14:6). But on the confession of Jesus Christ as Lord and Savior, we too are given keys to the kingdom (Matthew 16:19) to use to open the door for others to enter by faith.

What does verse 8 say Jesus has placed before this church?

_____.

Read Acts 14:27, 1 Corinthians. 16:9, 2 Corinthians 2:12, Colossians 4:3. What type of "open door" do these verses describe?

_____.

The scripture (verse 8) could infer that the opportunity for ministry was opened because of their deeds. Faithful obedience to God's Word and will provide the environment in which Christ, who is the Lord of the Harvest, can powerfully operate. The harvesting may be wrought with resistance, but through Christ we overcome; the door cannot be shut.

It may also be referring to their assurance of the open door of salvation that was theirs because of their deeds. We know they were faithful and obedient because Jesus said, "I know your deeds," yet had no words of rebuke. Jesus holds the key to salvation. When He unlocks the door for someone to enter, it cannot be closed.

They faced two obstacles. What difficulty does verse 8c express?

_____.

Although Christ had provided an open door, success would not come without opposition. Most commentators say that the church of Philadelphia was small, seemingly insignificant, without prestige or wealth. As such, perhaps they felt they were having very little impact or not as much as they had hoped. Based on Jesus's acknowledgment ("I know you have little strength,") it's clear that these believers were weary, exhausted from conflicts and the resistance to their mission.

The Lord knows when we're worn out, and He cares. There are many stories in Scripture that display His care and concern for the weary. What does Jesus promise those who are weary and burdened in Matthew 11:28–29?

_____.

Jesus invites us to bring all of our anxieties to Him because He cares for us (1 Peter 5:7). The work we're called to is too big for us alone. But in His strength, impossible things can happen, and God gets the glory.

The other obstacle appears to be a serious conflict between the Christians and those claiming to be Jews in Philadelphia. They were opposing the church and had shut the doors of the synagogue to the believers there. Jesus charges those who were falsely claiming to be Jews of belonging to the synagogue of Satan as he is the father of lies (John 8:44) and the source of all religious oppression (Ephesians 6:12).

What does Revelation 12:10b tell us about Satan and his activity?

_____.

Since Satan's mode of operation is accusations, we can most likely assume that he had incited the Jews to fabricate charges against the believers. You probably recall the hostility that the church in Smyrna underwent from the Jews in their city.

What had the church continued to do even in the face of adversarial conditions (verse 8c)?

_____

_____.

In spite of their weariness and, no doubt, discouragement, the church of Philadelphia had upheld a biblical standard and love for Christ. As opposed to some of the other churches who compromised their values and denied the Name of Christ, this church conducted themselves according the God's Word, thus glorifying His name.

Jesus makes three promises to this church. First, He will deal with their enemies.

Write Revelation 3:9b:

_____

_____.

Vengeance belongs to the Lord, and He promises to vindicate these believers before their antagonists. We know that a day is coming when everyone will acknowledge Christ as Lord (Philippians 2:10–11). Because He is holy and true and holds "the keys of death and Hades" (Revelation 1:18), He alone can pronounce judgment and close the door to heaven. But He may very well intend to destroy them _as_ enemies by using their admission of Christ's love toward us to reveal the truth that His love is available to them as well thereby opening the door to heaven for them to come.

Christ's second promise to them follows what God glorifying action on their part (verse 10a)?

_____

_____.

I suspect you may be familiar with this Greek word for _patient endurance_; it's _hupomeno_, and it means "to remain under"—that is, "to endure or sustain a load of miseries, adversities, persecutions, or provocations in faith and patience" (_The Complete Word Study New Testament_).

What are the things God has placed you or your church under that is a struggle to endure well?

_____

_____.

God has allowed the struggle for the purpose of maturity on our part and glory on His. What is the second promise (verse 10b)?

_____

_____.

The trial referenced here is the time of tribulation, described in Revelation 6–19, involving the entire earth before Jesus' return. There is much debate among scholars regarding the words "keep you from," and their opinions run the gamut on this subject. The question lies in deciding what exactly the phrase implies. Just to mention a few, a person holding to the pre-tribulationist view believes it to means that the church will be taken to heaven before the Tribulation period begins, and she will escape the trial altogether. The test is not for her but for unbelievers, most specifically the Jewish people. The mid-tribulationist views Scripture as saying believers will be raptured midway through the seven year period. As the second half of the tribulation will be horrific, this is the portion that the church will be rescued from. And post-tribulationists believe the rapture will occur at the end of the tribulation. They understand Scripture to say that the church will be preserved or kept from the trial by supernatural means of protection, but not delivered.

I (of course) have a solid opinion on it, but it's taken me years of consideration and investigation of Scripture to come to my conclusion. And even then, I wouldn't bet my life on it. As strong as it is, I'm prepared to be wrong. I encourage each of you to study it seriously for yourself and form your own opinion. What we can take with all certainty from Christ's words is (1) there will be a great trial over the entire earth and (2) Christ will provide for His bride. "The Lord knows those who are His" (2 Timothy 2:19b). I know, I know, I use this verse all the time, but I can't help it; I love it!

The third promise Jesus makes is to honor them. What distinction is made for the overcomers (verse 12)?

_____.

A pillar epitomizes stability, which would have been a wonderful assurance for the Philadelphia believers who understood the insecurity coming from the ever-present threat of ruin due to earthquakes. A pillar also symbolizes permanence. The Lord gives overcoming believers a permanent place in His temple in which they will never be forced out. In ancient time, great leaders were often honored by erecting a pillar with their name inscribed on it. Still today, we often use the term "pillars of the community" when describing a stable, hard-working person of character in society.

How are Peter, James and John referred to in Galatians 2:9a?

_____.

What three things will be written on this pillar (verse 12)?

_____

_____.

God's pillars are His faithful people who bear His name for His glory. This threefold promise pictures believers as belonging to God; His Name is eternally inscribed on our hearts and lives. We are citizens of heaven, the New Jerusalem, where we will reign with Christ, whom we will know by a "new name" (Revelation 19:12), a name that will unveil the full revelation of His character. 1 John 3:2 states, "When He appears, we shall be like Him, for we shall see Him as He is."

Day 5

The final message to the churches in Revelation is to the church of Laodicea. Read Revelation 3:14–22.

Laodicea was a wealthy city, known for its manufacture of rare black wool and a special eye salve. They had a famous temple to Asklepios, the god of healing, as well as a renowned medical school connected with the temple. The people of Laodicea were an independent group. When the city was destroyed by an earthquake, they refused Rome's offer of help and used their own resources for the reconstruction. The self-sufficient attitude had apparently permeated the church as well. This prosperous city had a major problem with their water supply; therefore, water had to be supplied from elsewhere.

How is Jesus revealed to the church of Laodicea (verse 14b)?

_____.

"Amen" is most often translated in Scripture as *verily* or *truly*, and it means firm or trustworthy. The word signals an acknowledgment of something as true and binding. So far, we have done a careful study of the true and binding work of Jesus Christ. All God's promises and covenants are fulfilled, guaranteed, and affirmed in Jesus Christ; He is the "Amen."

Jesus is the perfectly accurate and trustworthy witness to the truth of God. In addition, He will be faithful and true in what He witnesses. Jesus is the truth, and He speaks the truth.

Jesus is the beginning of all God's creation; rather, He is the source and ruler of God's creation.

Write John 1:3:

_____

_____.

What does Jesus know about their deeds (verse 15)?

_____.

What does Jesus threaten to do and why (verse 16)?

_____.

What type of person is Jesus referring to? What do the "temperatures" represent?

_____.

Many of us have been taught that the "hot" person is one on fire for Christ while the "cold" person is unsaved leaving the common understanding of "lukewarm" to be describing a believer who's become complacent, but I don't believe that could be the meaning.

What does Jesus say emphatically in verse 15b?

_____.

How could "cold" be descriptive of an unbeliever if Jesus said He wished it was their choice? This thought does not line up with the full counsel of God's Word. It is not His desire that any should perish; therefore, it's inconceivable that Christ would wish that people were spiritually cold if that meant unbelief.

To appreciate what Jesus is saying, we have to recognize the situation into which He speaks. Jesus uses the city's water supply problem as a parallel to the spiritual condition of the Laodicean church. Laodicea was located between Hieropolis, a city famous for their hot springs, and Colossae, who was known for their pure cold water. Water was transported via a six-mile aqueduct to Laodicea from Hieropolis, so by the time it reached Laodicea, it was no longer hot (or cold) but unappealingly lukewarm. The people had grown accustomed to it, but unsuspecting visitors immediately spit it out.

Water from the hot springs of Hieropolis was valuable in the comfort, relief, and healing it provided. Likewise, Colossae's icy-cold pure water was invigorating, bringing refreshment and thirst-quenching relief. The believers in Laodicea were lukewarm—indifferent, apathetic, and idle. They were providing neither comfort and healing nor refreshment and relief; they were useless. Jesus entreats them to recognize their lack of passion that had brought them to the place of ineffectiveness.

What are some of the ways the church can be like the hot springs of Hieropolis?

_____.

How might the church provide Colossae's pure icy-cold water?

_____.

The church is called to be like Christ who, as identified in this message, is the faithful and true witness. A lukewarm, useless church does not witness to the living Christ who meets the needs of all who come to Him.

As the true witness, Jesus tells them the truth about who they *actually* are as opposed to who they *say* they are.

This church says they are (verse 17a) _____.

This church was independent, self-satisfied, and secure: "We have need of nothing." They probably could have produced some great stats; i.e., large number of attendees, fat operating budgets, impressive staff. By all appearances, this was a healthy church.

But Jesus says they really are (17b) _____.

The problem in Laodicea was not just indifference; they were also ignorant of their real condition. In making the comparison, Jesus says, "but you do not realize." How is that possible? The difference is substantial; in fact, they're completely opposed. Ironically, the very things they were famous for and were self-sufficient in—wealth, cloth, eye salve—corresponded exactly to their needs spiritually. The church that had everything they needed was, in truth, afflicted and miserable. The source of their misery was blindness to their spiritual bankruptcy and nakedness before God.

The churches of both Laodicea and Sardis were complacent and ineffective for the purposes of Christ because of their wealth. Jesus found nothing commendable about either of them.

It was surely the rich material blessings the church enjoyed that caused them to say that they "do not need a thing." But these are dangerous words, as our very breath is dependent on Him. "He Himself gives all men life and breath and everything else" (Acts 17:25b). As ruler of creation, everything we have comes from Him. What is there to boast of? We are best served by the Beatitude of poor in spirit, recognizing our own poverty and desperation for God's grace toward us.

The Great Physician, in His grace, offers a remedy for the deadly spiritual condition of the Laodiceans. What advice does He give them (verse 18)?

_____
_____
_____.

All that the church in Laodicea thought they possessed in rich abundance, Jesus offers a genuine substitute for. The spiritually bankrupt can receive imperishable riches from Christ. In exchange for their fool's gold that held no eternal value, they can receive gold that's been refined.

Read 1 Peter 1:6–7. Based on these verses, what do you believe Jesus means in telling us to buy refined gold in which to become rich?

_____

_____

_____.

The church of Smyrna was called rich because they faithfully endured hardship and persecution. They didn't seek the worldly treasure they could have through compromise but trusted in God's promised rewards for His good and faithful servants. After all, as the above verses in 1 Peter affirm, it will be our faith, not our gold, on display when Christ returns.

The believers in Laodicea were dressing themselves with the beautiful, fine black wool the city manufactured. But like the emperor in Hans Christian Anderson's story "The Emperor's New Clothes," they were really naked. Christ exposes their nakedness and shame. He offers them white robes made from His own righteousness as a covering.

What is the exchange in Isaiah 1:18? "Though your sins are like scarlet, they shall be _____; though they are crimson, they shall become like _____."

The church was completely blind to their true spiritual condition and for that, their famous eye salve was useless. But Jesus opens the eyes of the blind. It's so easy to see areas of sin in the lives of others but often so difficult to see in our own; we're blind to them. Jesus offers the antidote. By looking intently into the mirror of His Word, fully illuminated, magnifying His holiness and righteousness, His Spirit will reveal the things in our lives that need to be removed. Jesus also gives eyes to see our future hope; by His Spirit, He reveals the unseen, unheard of, and inconceivable (1 Corinthians 2:9).

Although the church of Laodicea present Jesus with nothing in which He might praise them, He loves this church.

Write Revelation 3:19:

_____.

It sounds to me like His words infer that there was rebuke and discipline going on in this church. Perhaps they were begrudging His divinely appointed trials or hardships and the effort of refinement was futile. God reminds them that discipline is an expression of His love; it is a grace. While we so easily lose sight of the goal, Jesus is ever mindful of what's at stake. We must not resist His discipline. Like any good father, God cares about our character.

What does Hebrews 12:5–7 and 10b say about God's discipline and rebuke?

_____.

What does lack of disciple signify (Hebrews12:8)?

_____.

We should never fear the Lord's discipline; it's when He stops showing us where we're coming off the track that we need to be really concerned! Jesus calls for earnestness and zeal.

What does Romans 12:11 tell us never to be lacking in?

_____.

Spiritual fervor and zealousness for the things of God rekindle the fire in our hearts to lead us to repent of self-righteousness, sin and apathy. What image is given of Jesus (Revelation 3:20a)?

_____.

Imagine this picture—Jesus presents Himself ("Here I am!") and knocks at the door, *our* door. Why in the world would He knock? We were told in the message to Philadelphia that He holds the key; why wouldn't He just let Himself in? Besides, He has purchased us, so the house is His. Do you knock on the door of your own house? You may have heard this verse used in reference to an evangelical call to an unbeliever, and while He does draw men to Himself, that is not the picture here. This message is to the church; Jesus stands at the door of His bride seeking entrance!

What does Jesus say in verse 20b?

_____
_____.

According to this verse, what's the first thing that has to happen before the door can be open?

_____.

In spite of Jesus's rightful ability to impose His presence on us, He doesn't, but He does knock. The issue is, do we hear. From the beginning, the emphasis of these messages has been to hear. Allow Jesus the opportunity to take your face in His hands, directing your eyes to His, and hear Him say; "Listen to me."

What instruction does Hebrews 12:25 give us regarding Jesus speaking?

_____.

The word translated as *refuse* means to beg to be excused, to decline, or refuse the thing spoken of, avoid.

Jesus knocks at the door of His bride, your door. He's pursuing you. His desire is to spend time with you, to hear what's going on in your life, to empower you for His work, to take your fears and anxieties, to show you great and unsearchable things you don't know, to warn you of dangerous alliances, to enlighten, inspire, and reveal His awesome splendor. For heaven's sake, answer the door!

We have all had times when we've chosen to ignore Jesus's knocking, pretending we didn't hear. What have been some of your reasons?

_____
_____
_____.

Does the picture of Jesus literally standing outside knocking change your perspective and make you less likely to disregard Him? Why or Why not?

_____
_____
_____.

As those called by His Name, we cannot assume His presence; we have to open the door and invite Him in—not in order for Him to see what we're doing, but for us to see and know what He's doing so we can join Him.

What promise is given to those who overcome the sin of pride, self-sufficiency, and apathy (verse 21)?

_____.

These are Jesus's final word to His bride; the letters contain His personal encouragement to His beloved to hold tight to her faith until He comes; we will not be disappointed that we did. The day is coming when everyone will see the church for what she really is: the precious and beautiful bride of Jesus.

> The Bride of Christ is a sort of Cinderella now, sitting among the ashes. She is like her Lord, 'despised and rejected of men'; the watchmen smite her, and take away

her veil from her; for they know her not, even as they knew not her Lord. But when he shall appear, then shall she appear also, and in his glorious manifestation she also shall shine forth as the sun in the kingdom of the Father. (Spurgeon)

SUMMARY

Church	Commendation	Rebuke	Action
Ephesus	Worked hard, persevered, Intolerant of evil	Forsake first love	Turn back to Christ.
Smyrna	Suffered persecution and poverty	None	Don't fear.
Pergamum	Remained true to the faith	Idolatry and immorality	Repent.
Thyatira	Acted in love and faith	Tolerated false teaching, immoral idolatrous	Hold on to what they had.
Sardis	None	Spiritually dead	Remember and wake up.
Philadelphia	Remained faithful	None	Hold on to what they had.
Laodicea	None	Lukewarm	Open the door.

THE HOLY WEDDING

Summary

What a beautiful picture God has woven for us all through His Word to display His immeasurable love and desire for His people. Solomon's words are true: who can fathom what God has done from beginning to end (Ecclesiastes 3:11c).

Through our study, the love of God was revealed as so vast it cannot be contained, so He created mankind in which to share it. We saw Him call out a nation to take to Himself in which they would be His people and He would be their God. We saw His faithfulness love, hesed, displayed to them even in their adultery. We witnessed the coming of Christ to fulfill the covenant and pay the bride price in order to redeem His people and produce a beautiful, unblemished, unstained bride for Himself. Jesus has returned to the Father and is preparing a place for us. He has left us His Holy Spirit to enable us to be prepared for His return. And so here we are.

Soon, God the Father will give the word, and whether individually or collectively, Jesus will come for His bride. The time is ripe for the holy wedding.

"So you also must be ready, because the Son of Man will come at an hour when you do not expect him" (Matthew 24:44).

"Now, brothers, about times and dates we do not need to write to you, for you know very well that the day of the Lord will come like a thief in the night. While people are saying, 'Peace and safety,' destruction will come on them suddenly, as labor pains on a pregnant woman, and they will not escape. But you, brothers, are not in darkness so that this day should surprise you like a thief. You are all son of the light and sons of the day. We do not belong to the night or to the darkness. So then, let us not be like others, who are asleep, but let us be alert and self-controlled" (1 Thessalonians 5:1–6).

These scriptures state that everyone will be surprised at Christ's return. For some it will be a good surprise, but for others it will not. Consider something with me for a moment—when is it that we don't enjoy or appreciate a surprise? Isn't it when you feel ill-prepared or unready? Let's say your friend/child/spouse has planned and executed an elaborate surprise party for you with all those you care about in attendance. What could be better? You, unsuspecting of the activities going on, are lured to this magnificent party after having worked in the yard all day in what is certainly not your best look. This, of course, is not going to produce the happy, delighted, welcome response hoped for no matter how extravagant the party. Why? Because you were not prepared. Preparedness has everything to do with how we respond to a surprise.

Therefore, Scripture reminds us again and again to be alert, ready, and expecting the appearance of our Bridegroom. Jesus states clear that He is coming like a thief. How does a thief come? Unannounced!

We are certain of Jesus's return, and based on God's Word and the traditions of a Jewish wedding that He holds so closely to, we can expect to be surprised—but not alarmed. Our reaction will be delight, not distress.

In Matthew 24:37–41 and correspondingly Luke 17:26–29, Jesus compares the time of His return to the days of Noah and Lot. What did both of these times have in common? Prevailing wickedness, so much so that only a small few (a remnant) were considered righteous. In both these instances, it was "business as usual." Sam Storms in his book *Kingdom Come* expresses it this way: "Humanity will be immersed in the routine affairs of life—like in the days of Noah and Lot, and therefore the world will be caught completely off-guard by Christ's coming as people go about their everyday routines and activities. Jesus will come at a time of wide-spread indifference, normalcy, materialistic endeavors, when everyone is involved in the pursuit of their earthy affairs and ambitions (2 Peter 3:3–4, 5). Jesus will come at a time when His coming is the farthest thing from people's minds."

As people were eating, drinking, marrying, buying and selling, planting, etc., disaster fell. In each case, God warned of judgment, God removed the righteous, and God followed through with judgment. What I think needs to get our attention is the finality of it—when it's over, it's over!

I've always been struck by the words of Genesis 7:16. Once Noah, his family, and all the animals had entered the ark, the verse says, "Then the Lord shut Him in." Imagine for a moment Noah's position: the water was rising swiftly, and people were running to the refuge of the ark. This was a godly man, so we have to know his desire was to help! But it was not up to him. The door that would have provided salvation from the flood waters was closed by God, not Noah. We too are mercifully not given the duty of shutting the door of salvation to others. That's God's to do alone.

We saw in Christ's message to the church of Philadelphia that He alone opens and shuts the door of opportunity. While it is open, we need to tell others about Christ. Revelation 22:17 states, "The Spirit and the bride say, 'Come!'" But do we? Do we cry out to others to come to Jesus? Or are we indifferent or too busy readying ourselves? Drawing others to Christ is part of our readiness. The writer of Hebrews said that Jesus endured the horrors of the cross for the joy set before Him—which was making a way for His bride to join Him in His kingdom. That should be the same joy that drives us to openly share the gospel. How can we happily anticipate the delightful surprise of Christ's appearing, knowing that for unbelievers, some of which surely comprise people you know and love, that day will be one of sudden and unexpected destruction?

It might be tremendously helpful to keep the following picture in your mind: Imagine yourself on the ark as the waters begin to quickly rise. It suddenly dawns on the unsuspecting that destruction is at hand, and panic and chaos ensues. One of those is your neighbor, sister, dad, cousin, or best friend. You stand safely inside the ark while the waters around that person you love swiftly begin to overtake them. Your eyes meet; theirs plead with you for help. Of course, you want to reach out and rescue them. You wouldn't even have to like this person! But God shuts the door; the opportunity has passed and is no longer available. Listen, it will be that final; the time is now.

Scripture tells us the Lord takes no pleasure in the death of the wicked (Ezekiel 33:11); His desire is that all would receive salvation. I would suspect that in Noah's day, when he first began to build the ark, it got the people's attention. They were probably heeding the warning of upcoming disaster, but as time went on and nothing happened, they went back to life as usual. In the same way, the attitude in society today seems to be just as that described in 2 Peter 3:4 when people were saying, "Where is this 'coming' he promised." Peter responds to that with: "The Lord is not slow in keeping his promise, as some understand slowness. He is patient with you not wanting anyone to perish, but everyone to come to repentance. But the day of the Lord will come like a thief. The heavens will disappear with a roar; the elements will be destroyed by fire, and the earth and everything in it will be laid bare. Since everything will be destroyed in this way, what kind of people ought you to be?" (2 Peter 3:9–11)

That's a great question. As earlier noted, Scripture continually refers to Christ's coming as a thief. Besides secrecy, what does a thief do? He takes. Likewise, everything in this world will be taken; we will be stripped of all worldly goods. The person who has spent their life investing in money, reputation, hobbies, or pleasure will stand before God utterly shamed and naked as it will have all been burned away. But the life invested and devoted to the things that will last has nothing of value for the thief to steal; their treasure is stored in heaven. Listen to 1 Corinthians 15:51–58:

> Listen, I tell you a mystery: We will not all sleep, but we will all be changed—in a flash, in the twinkling of an eye, at the last trumpet. For the trumpet will sound, the dead will be raised imperishable, and we will be changed. For the perishable must clothe itself with the imperishable, and the mortal with immortality When the perishable has been clothed with the imperishable, and the mortal with immortality, then the saying that is written will come true:
>
> "Death has been swallowed up in victory."
>
> "Where, O death, is your victory? Where, O death, is your sting?"
>
> The sting of death is sin, and the power of sin is the law. But thanks be to God! He gives us the victory through our Lord Jesus Christ.

What an amazing salvation we have been given! What an amazing Savior!

"Though you have not seen him, you love him; and even though you do not see him now, you believe in him and are filled with an inexpressible and glorious joy, for you are receiving the goal of your faith, the salvation of your souls" (1 Peter 1:8–9).

It says, "You *are* receiving." It's already happening. The Lord will complete the good work He began in you. The incredible gift of salvation should evoke immense joy. If it doesn't, then we've lost sight of what we've been saved from. We haven't been saved just from slavery to sin, just death, or even just hell. We've been saved from the wrath of God! And if that doesn't stir up some strong emotions, then we need to revisit Jesus's path to the cross—not just his death on the cross but all the horror leading to that point in order to remember what it looks as God's wrath falls on a person.

"Therefore, my dear brothers, stand firm. Let nothing move you. Always give yourselves fully to the work of the Lord, because you know that your labor in the Lord is not in vain" (1 Corinthians 15:58).

No, it's not in vain; in fact, our labor in the Lord (otherwise known as the righteous acts of the saints) will be the very thing God uses to make our beautiful white garment—our wedding gown in which we will be presented to Him.

"Then I heard what sounded like a great multitude, like the roar of rushing waters and like loud peals of thunder, shouting: 'Hallelujah! For our Lord God Almighty reigns. Let us rejoice and be glad and give him glory! For the wedding of the Lamb has come and his bride has made herself ready. Fine linen, bright and clean, was given her to wear'" (Revelation 19:6–9a).

As part of the wedding custom, the bride and groom consummate the union by the physical act of sex. The consummation of our marriage to Christ is and is not similar.

The physical consummation of a marriage is one of deep intimacy, pointing to a greater spiritual consummation between Christ and His bride. The Hebrew word that is used to convey the physical act of sex is *yada*, which means "to know" in the sense of experiential knowledge. When a man and woman come together, the Bible says they become one. That is as close to "knowing" a person as we have here. When we stand before Christ as the bride to the Bridegroom, the veil will finally be completely removed, and we will experience depth of intimacy and full knowledge. What great joy we should possess as we await the consummation of this wedding.

"Now we see but a poor reflection as in a mirror, then we shall see face to face. Now I know in part; then I shall know fully, even as I am fully known" (1 Corinthians 13:12).

"But we know that when he appears, we shall be like him, for we shall see him as he is" 1 John 3:2b.

The focus of the wedding ceremony most often is on the bride, but not this one; all eyes will be locked on the Bridegroom! And we will join with all the others around His throne crying: "Holy, holy, holy is the Lord God Almighty, who was, and is, and is to come."

"Then I saw a new heaven and a new earth, for the first heaven and the first earth had passed away, and there was no longer any sea. I saw the Holy City, the New Jerusalem, coming down out of heaven for God, prepared as a bride beautifully dressed for her husband. And I heard a loud voice from the throne say, 'Now the dwelling of God is with men, and he will live with them. They will be his people, and God himself will be with them and be their God. He will wipe every tear from their eyes. There will be no more death or mourning or crying or pain, for the old order of things has passed away.' He said to me: 'It is done. I am the Alpha and the Omega, the Beginning and the End. To him who is thirsty I will give to drink without cost from the spring of water of life. He who overcomes will inherit *all this*, and I will be his God and he will be my son" (Revelation 21:1–7, emphasis mine).

God promises us "all this!" Imagine what John must have seen as he is told that overcomers would inherit "all this!" What then is worth clinging tightly to here in comparison to what we've been promised?

As we look to that promise of a new heaven and a new earth where only righteousness will exist and in which the glory and excellence of God will cover the earth—and we *relish* that promise and *hope* in that promise—a divine power fires us with a zeal for purity as we wait for His coming.

"Blessed are those who are called to the marriage supper of the Lamb!" (Revelation 19:9)

Blessed indeed! Jesus Himself eagerly anticipates this marriage supper. He spoke longingly of the day when He will drink of the fruit of the vine again, with His disciples in the kingdom (Matthew 26:29).

"The City Harmonic (Feat. JJ Heller)—Holy (Wedding Day) (Official Music Video)."
https://www.youtube.com/watch?v=k8YMn_7lFu8

Holy (Wedding Day)
The City Harmonic

This is the story of the Son of God
Hanging on the cross for me
But it ends with a bride and groom
And a wedding by a glassy sea
O death where is your sting
'Cause I'll be there singing
Holy Holy Holy
Is the Lord

This is the story of a bride in white
Waiting on her wedding day
Anticipation welling up inside
While the groom is crowned as king
O death where is your sting
'Cause we'll be there singing
Holy Holy Holy is the Lord

Holy Holy Holy Holy Holy Holy
Is the Lord Almighty
Holy Holy Holy Holy Holy Holy
Is the Lord Almighty
Who was and is and is to come
Who was and is and is to come

This is the story of the Son of God
Hanging on the cross for me
And it ends with a bride and groom
And a wedding by a glassy sea

This is the story of the a bride in white
Singing on her wedding day
Of the God who was and is to stand before a bride who sings
Holy Holy Holy Holy Holy Holy is the Lord Almighty

REFERENCE

egrc.net, "The God of the Covenant" by Lois Tverberg.

Followtherabbi.com, various articles.

A Christian Love Story, Zola Levitt.

Fire on the Mountain, Discovery Guide and DVD, Ray Vander Laan.

Messianicfellowship.50webs.com, "Jewish Wedding Customs and the Bride of Messiah," Glenn Kay.

"Why Did God Create Humanity?" by Greg Brezina, Christian Families Today

"Fire on the Mountain," Ray Vander Laan,

followtherabbi.com, "A Covenant Guarantee" by Ray Vander Laan

"Irony in the Extreme," Lois Tverberg, egrc.net

"Systematic Theology," Wayne Grudem

"Vertical Church," James MacDonald

"Walking in the Dust of Rabbi Jesus," Lois Tverberg

"The MacArthur Bible Commentary," John MacArthur

NIV Bible Commentary

"The Bible among the Myths," John Oswalt

"Is Jesus in the Old Testament?" Iain Duguid

"The God Who Smokes," Timothy Stoner

"A Knowledge of the Holy," A. W. Tozer

"The Expulsive Power of a New Affection," Thomas Chalmers

David Guzik Commentary, blueletterbible.org

"Revelation: Unlocking the Future, Edward Hindson

The Seat of Satan: Ancient Pergamum, by Gordon Robertson

A Light in the Darkness, Rick Renner

"A Commentary on the Revelation of John," George Eldon Ladd

The Complete Word Study New Testament

"The Marriage of the Lamb," Charles Spurgeon

"Kingdom Come," Sam Storm

ABOUT THE AUTHOR

Kim Huff, a Christian teacher and speaker, fervently seeks to know and perceive Jesus through the written word of God. There is no greater tragedy in her mind than for a reader to walk away from the Scriptures with anything but awe and admiration for a God so compelling. Her zeal for the church, Christ's bride, to personally experience the wonders of Christ through His written Word is exposed in her expressive style of teaching. Kim lives with her husband, Don, in Houston, Texas, and is fortunate to have her grown children, Khara and Trenton, and their families in the same city.